LANCASHIRE
·V·
HITLER

LANCASHIRE
·V·
HITLER

Civilians at War

Ron Freethy

COUNTRYSIDE BOOKS
NEWBURY BERKSHIRE

First published 2006
© Ron Freethy 2006

COUNTRYSIDE BOOKS
3 Catherine Road,
Newbury, Berkshire.

To view our complete range of books,
please visit us at
www.countrysidebooks.co.uk

ISBN 1 84674 008 8
EAN 978 184674 008 4

Designed by Peter Davies, Nautilus Design
Produced through MRM Associates Ltd, Reading
Printed by Woolnough Bookbinding Ltd., Irthlingborough.

CONTENTS

County Map of Lancashire
1939 - 1945

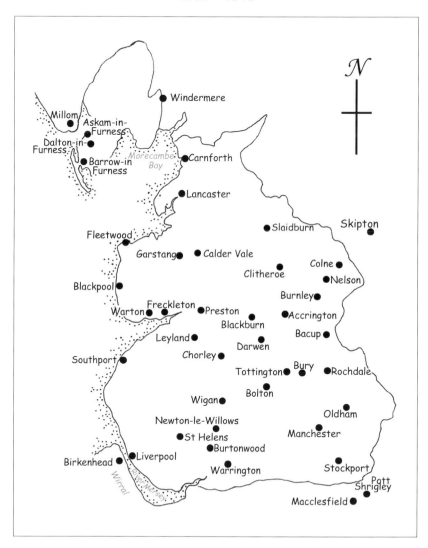

Introduction

The people of Lancashire during the war had stories to tell which should never be forgotten. While the army, navy and air force concentrated on the battlefields of Europe and the Far East, civilians were intent upon defending themselves and their families from bombing raids, growing their own food to supplement the meagre rations, and, in the case of many children and some adults, adjusting to life as evacuees far from home. Armaments had to be produced, industry kept rolling, and military buildings and airfields constructed, a process which accelerated when the Americans came into the war after 1941, crossing the Atlantic Bridge to Liverpool. The transport system had to be kept going too, and was worked almost, but fortunately not quite, to breaking point. All these essential services had to be provided by civilians and their contribution to the winning of the war is often not fully appreciated or documented.

This is not an academic book but one that is made up of the personal memories of those who went through this traumatic period in Lancashire. As I was completing my book *Lancashire: The Secret War*, it became obvious that I had received lots of photographs and letters from people who were not concerned with secret invasion or defensive plans, but who nevertheless had a very special tale to tell – this is their story.

Ron Freethy

Acknowledgements

I **received so much help** that it is hard to thank everyone for their contribution. Many are named along with their memories but there are a number of individuals who have taken the trouble to provide me with contacts as well as information.

I extend my thanks to Lancashire's newspaper editors who printed my requests for information. To the editorial staff of the *Lancashire Evening Telegraph*, led by John Anson, I owe a special thanks.

Museums have been a constant source of information and their exhibits relating to the war are listed in the appendix of the book. Three tourist steam railways have provided me with invaluable information – the East Lancashire Railway, the Keighley and Worth Valley Railway and the Embsay and Bolton Abbey Railway. All have locomotives and rolling stock dating to the Second World War and are a useful historical archive.

Andrew Mann of BAe Systems has given generously of his time and provided me with many contacts as well as providing advice with regard to context. To my cousin, Alan Hargreaves, I am grateful for hospitality and advice and to my friends Eric Riley and Betty Parton I give thanks for memories and suggestions.

To the staff of Countryside Books I give thanks for their encouragement. Nicholas Battle first suggested this project and he has given me encouragement throughout the gestation period of this volume. To my wife, Marlene, I owe a real debt of thanks for producing a manuscript from my handwriting.

Chapter 1

The Bomber Will Always Get Through

In 1932 the Prime Minister, Stanley Baldwin, put into chilling words what everyone in military circles was coming to accept, that 'the bomber will always get through'. The population had to come to terms with the changing nature of war and the fact that they could be directly targeted from the air. The bombing of civilians in Shanghai by the Japanese in 1932, and the German perfection of dive-bombing technqiues during the Spanish Civil War and subsequently in Poland in 1939, with Junkers Ju 87s (known as Stukas) creating mayhem and terror, all underlined the prophetic words of Baldwin. In the event of war, our cities would have to face the very real threat from squadrons of enemy bombers. On 3rd September 1939 Britain declared war on Germany and the threat became a reality.

Yet most people in Lancashire in 1939 thought that the county was far too remote from the Continent to be at great risk and that German bombers would not be able to reach them. It is amazing how often people fail to take notice of history. During the First World War the Kaiser's Zeppelins had caused loss of life in Lancashire – if the county was in range at that time, then the Luftwaffe should not have a problem. On 25th September 1916 a Zeppelin dropped its first incendiary bomb on Newchurch; it proved to be a dud but at least it reached its target. On went the airship, to cross the East Lancashire Railway (now operated as a steam-hauled tourist attraction) and create a small amount of damage. The Zeppelin then reached Bolton and dropped a string of bombs, which destroyed 19 houses, killed 13 people and injured many others. Eighteen months later, on 12th April 1918, another Zeppelin bombed Wigan and killed five people. On each of these occasions the German crews returned safely to base. These two sorties ought to have convinced the defence planners that Lancashire's vital industries needed to be protected but the lessons of history were not properly learned.

Even after war had been declared, the authorities were slow to react. Air raid warnings which sounded on 25th June 1940 proved that the bombers could get through. Not even bombs dropped close to a searchlight unit at Altcar near Liverpool on the nights of 28th and 29th July, nor a more damaging raid near the Tranmere football ground at Birkenhead on 9th August, resulted in any meaningful defensive action.

Over the inter-war years aircraft design had improved almost beyond recognition. The new bombers were huge in size and range in comparison with their First World War ancestors, whilst the boffins had been busy designing bigger and more effective bombs. These were to be specifically aimed at civilian targets, especially those areas involved in the armament industry, and around docklands. It is interesting to note that Germany never managed to produce a four-engined bomber and this omission certainly reduced

In view of the close proximity to army and air force stations it is surprising that Blackpool was not systematically bombed. On 12 September 1940, however, houses in Seed Street were demolished by a bomb.

Was Blackpool right to worry about German bombing? It would seem to be the case, as this photograph shows. It was taken from the German War Ministry files and marks the Blackpool airfields and factories.

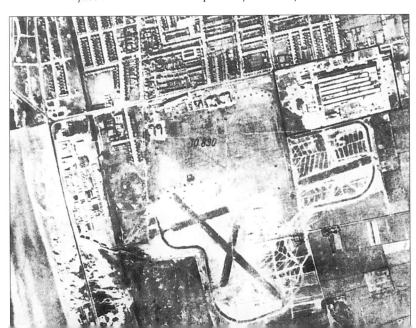

damage to British cities and civilians. Four engines meant more power and therefore the ability to drop more and heavier bombs.

It has been shown that although large high explosive bombs were both spectacular from the attacker's point of view and terrifying for those on the receiving end, it was actually the incendiary that did the most physical damage. The conception that the incendiary was just there to create a target fire to guide the bombers in is altogether wrong, although this may well have been their original function.

Basically the incendiary consisted of a cylinder of magnesium inside which was a core of thermite. This was mainly composed of aluminium and iron oxide, thus producing a highly effective firework-like weapon, burning for a few minutes at a temperature of around 3,000°C.

This type of incendiary had to be dealt with quickly before any fire took hold and industrial and residential properties were provided with buckets of sand and stirrup pumps. Civilians had to take the lead here and training had to be given, though most people thought that these instructions were just stating the obvious. Wills Tobacco Company joined in by issuing a series of Home Defence Cigarette Cards, which have now become collector's items.

WILLS'S CIGARETTES

THE STIRRUP HAND PUMP

Many air raid sirens were hand-operated but few remain in working order like the one pictured here. A handle was attached to the screw on the left.

It took courage, however, to try to deal with a spluttering device looking so much like the fizzing bomb of comic fiction. Once alight it ignited furniture and all wooden structures and it was these resultant fires which caused more civilian casualties than the high explosive missiles. This put great pressure on the fire services. Incendiaries were later modified by German scientists with the specific intention of increasing civilian casualties. One variation was the addition of phosphorus, initially confined in glass phials. These shattered on impact and the oil and rubber used in the bomb linings generated a burning liquid which caused horrendous injuries.

Another German invention which the Civil Defence authorities had to deal with was the aerial or parachute bomb. These weapons, which floated slowly down and exploded on impact, were dropped around the docks and shipping lanes. The idea was to increase the time over which explosions took place. These were highly effective and caused plenty of damage when they impacted against buildings.

Those on fire duty in dockland areas were given warning

This photograph, taken in 1939, shows the Lancashire sense of humour. Close to Piccadilly Station, Manchester, men are working hard building a surface air raid shelter. In the background is a notice reading 'Don't Let Rupture Stop You Digging For Victory'! The horse and cart on the right underline the vital part that horsepower played in transport during this period.

of these weapons but not everybody appreciated either the size or their explosive power, as Ted Ousby of Barrow-in-Furness recalled: 'I was on fire duty on the roof of the post office along with others, one of whom was not very bright. He brought with him a piece of home-designed equipment which he said would deal with any "air bomb" as he called it. This device was made from a clothes prop with a sweeping brush secured to the end. After struggling up the stairs with his long and clumsy device he proceeded to demonstrate how he intended to chase the German bomb and fend it off with his brush!' This provided lots of fun and it was the British sense of humour which prevailed at this time, although the real danger soon became very evident.

In truth, however, it is difficult to see what more could have been done. By 1940, London, the South East and the Midlands were already stretched to the limit with the Blitz in full swing. The Germans were bombing at night and with radar in its infancy the detection of enemy aircraft was all but impossible. Some of the early experimental radar installations sprouted from Blackpool Tower early in 1940. Lancashire at that time had very few fighter aircraft available for defence and most of these were obsolete. This gave the Luftwaffe pilots almost carte blanche and at this time it is easy to appreciate just how vital were the blackout regulations.

Liverpool and Manchester were the most important targets and if these cities could not be located then the Luftwaffe crews were allowed to jettison their bombs to lighten their load. The bombers were often operating at the limit of their fuel range. To Lancastrians on the ground it became difficult to establish whether the Germans were aiming at specific targets or were just reducing excess weight.

German raids on Liverpool Docks began on 17th and 18th August 1940 but in retrospect these can now be regarded as 'sighting sorties'. The Germans were hard at work developing aircraft

Radar masts sprouting from Blackpool Tower.

with a longer range and capable of carrying either more or heavier bombs. No aircraft was capable of what we now define as precision bombing and the answer was to indulge in blanket bombing with no thought given to the civilian population.

This 'blitz' hit London first, then Coventry, and eventually Manchester and Liverpool. There is no doubt that Christmas 1940 should go down as one of the blackest days in Manchester's history. Dennis Wood of the Manchester Police Museum recorded that: 'On Christmas Eve 1940 Manchester was attacked by a large force of German bombers, which went on until dawn on Christmas Day. Records show that between the 22nd and 25th of December 1,005 people were killed and many more were injured. This compares to the 4,100 Liverpool people who were killed between 1940 and 1941 and the 1,236 poor folk who were killed in Coventry. Luftwaffe records show that 150 aircraft were involved in the Manchester raids.'

During the Christmas period of 1941 what must be one of the worst examples on record of public relations took place in Manchester. Dennis Wood recalled for me this sad chapter: 'On Christmas Eve 1941 crowds of Mancunians swarmed around the shops in Market Street and Deansgate. They had little cash to spend and rationing of almost everything curtailed anything which might be regarded as a spree. Some of the big stores had attempted to make an effort to brighten up their window displays but potential shoppers had to make certain to take a look before dark because of course, due to the blackout, the windows could not be illuminated. Fresh in everyone's mind was the awful bombing of the previous year when the blitz had taken such a toll. Following that horrendous period the bombing had eased and the people were beginning to relax.

'At 3 o'clock in the afternoon, three twin-engined bombers flew low over Piccadilly and Market Street. When the shoppers looked up they saw that the bomb doors of the

The aircraft dropping leaflets in the Manchester hoax of 1941.
(Below) Civilians reading one of the leaflets.

aircraft were open and objects were falling from each aircraft. Everyone dashed to find shelter fearing that bombs were falling. In the rush several people including some children were injured, some being run over by vehicles.

'It soon became apparent that there were no explosions and what were fluttering into the crowd were leaflets printed in red and bearing a message from the Chief Constable to the effect that everybody should take extra care on the roads over the holiday, as this was the time of the year, especially during the blackout, that there were a lot of accidents.

'The Chairman of the Watch Committee, when asked by the press to account for the insensitivity of the exercise, said that he had not been informed of the event. It all came down to an inspector who had close friends in the RAF and decided to drop the leaflets on the city. The Lord Mayor stated that he had had no notification of the plan and was actually laying a wreath at the communal grave of the 1940 victims at the precise time of the leaflet drop. The Mayor said, "It might have been wise to have given some warning to the public before carrying out the leaflet drop." '

This was an understatement if ever there was one, but there must have been a great deal of pre-planning because photographs of the leaflet-dropping bombers were taken, as were shots of civilians reading the leaflets. What had not been properly thought out was the insensitive disregard for the feelings of those who grieved for the dead or perhaps were injured themselves during the 1940 raid. No wonder there was a mini panic.

The memories of people involved in the real blitz was still fresh in the minds of those involved, as Terry Perkins who still lives in the Burnage district of the city recalls: 'The first night of the bombing was heralded by the sinister drone of enemy aircraft and suddenly the sky lit up and there was a deafening roar as the first bombs came crashing down. After the aircraft had gone we heard the tinkle of glass as the occupants of the streets began the unpleasant task of

The traditional rivalry between Manchester United and Manchester City football teams was forgotten when Old Trafford was bombed. Both teams played at City's ground, then at Maine Road, until long after the war.

sweeping up. Stepping into this we almost skated on the glass and powdered rubble. Hardly a house had escaped intact. We were lucky having only the rear windows blown out of our house. I remember a real sense of space. Whole streets of terraced houses lay in ruins with the smoke of still burning buildings curling up into the sky. We could see the huge gasometer in Miles Platting fully revealed for the first time, which had remarkably escaped the bombs.

'At the bottom of our street a whole family had been wiped out and we watched as bodies, including that of a baby, were loaded into a lorry. In a curious and detached way seeing this horror, we kids still did not feel personally threatened. These horrors only happened to other people.

'On the following night I was in an air-raid shelter and

19

A bomb fell in Ainsworth Street, Blackburn, on 31 August 1940. The civilians are going about their normal business and one man is smoking without any thought of possible gas leaks.

just after the all clear sounded we heard a swishing noise and then silence. Later I went into the house and we were making a brew of tea. Almost as soon as I started to carry the tea there was a terrific explosion. The house rocked and I dropped the tea. The swishing sound had been a delayed action parachute bomb. When it exploded it wiped out half of a street only a hundred yards away from our house.'

Damage to Manchester city centre was extensive. The cathedral was all but destroyed and the Free Trade Hall also received a direct hit. All that was left standing was a façade of the once proud headquarters of the famous Hallé Orchestra. Since 2005 this façade has become a feature of the impressive and newly constructed Radisson Hotel on Deansgate.

There is no doubt that fires following the explosions or caused by incendiaries were a major threat. The Fire Brigade had real problems when water mains were hit and, to counteract this, temporary ponds filled with water were constructed close to many large and important buildings.

Dennis Wood recalls that he lived close to Heaton Park, in which batteries of anti-aircraft guns were established to defend Manchester: 'I think there were about 150 guns in the park. When the Germans changed their tactics in 1940 from using their air force to destroy ours, in preparation for an invasion, to targeting civilians, those guns came into almost nightly use. When, as was regularly the case, all the guns in the park were firing the noise was tremendous and went on for long periods. When they stopped we could still hear them vibrating in our ears for a further five minutes or so. I read in later years that the guns did little to bring down enemy planes but were meant to be a morale booster.'

Dennis Wood, Dave Tetlow and Duncan Broady of the Police Museum in Manchester allowed me to look at beat constables' notebooks written during the war. Each bobby carried a set of keys for the communal shelters in his area. When the alarm sounded he unlocked the shelter and after

Blackpool took its air raid precautions seriously. In 1939 a huge shelter was built along the Golden Mile stretch of the promenade.

the 'all clear' he had to remove people such as courting couples and vagrants before locking up again to ensure that the shelter remained fit to be occupied. These notebooks also reveal the names and addresses of those who had lights showing during the blackout. The number of bulbs glowing and also their wattage were accurately noted and many people were summonsed.

The first major attack on Liverpool came on 28th November 1940 when a two and a half hour barrage killed 200 people. Things got much worse during May 1941, when 3,966 people were killed, 3,812 were seriously injured, 10,000 buildings were destroyed and a further 184,000 damaged.

The rubble was cleared to allow life around the docks to go on; much was dumped along the river bank around what is now the Otterspool promenade and some was taken to the Hightown area on the way to Southport. These humps and bumps eventually grassed over and are now a highly regarded if unofficial nature reserve.

In July 1980 I interviewed the famous Lancashire writer Miss Jessica Lofthouse and I am glad that I kept a record of what she told me with regard to the bombing of Liverpool: 'May turned out to be a real problem because the Germans hit us hard in 1940 and again in 1941. I remember seeing Venus rising bright among a ring of barrage balloons above the Pier Head. Then searchlights stabbed out into the night and the bombers came over. I saw hospital ships in the river, and men injured during the Dunkirk evacuation in 1940 passed through Lime Street station and many were transferred on to Aintree Racecourse, which looked like a tented city.

'In 1941 the Germans came again and I can remember the docks being ablaze for days and at night many people went out into the local countryside and slept more safely in the woods. I remember one old lady saying to me, "My son is building bombers near Manchester. At least we will be able to get our own back."'

This spirit was evident during these dark days and the Lancashire humour shone brightly through the Blitz as Mr Arthur Ainsworth, now living in Burnley, recalled: 'I was working in an aeroplane factory near Manchester when over the tannoy came an announcement that joiners and builders working in the factory were urgently needed in Liverpool to repair bomb damage. I put my name down and was accepted. I had to be up at six in the morning for an eight o'clock start. I worked in the Sefton area where the damage was really bad. We repaired houses using what materials we could find. I have seen bodies being pulled out of the rubble; some had been blown up through chimney flues, which were only nine inches square. I got talking to a young lady who told me that she was in bed when a parachute mine landed near to her house. The explosion lifted her and her bed through the roof and into the middle of the street. There was not a mark on her and so she was one of the lucky ones.

'These Liverpool folk had a wonderful sense of humour. I went into a bomb-damaged house. In the centre of the room was a sideboard surrounded by shattered glass. The front door and the windows had been blasted out. In the midst of this wreckage sat a young woman breast-feeding her child. She grinned at my surprise and said, "What do you want? Have you not 'ad your breakfast?" '

Obviously the spirit of survival burned bright during this time but there was no defence against a direct hit. Long before the war, however, the best design for air raid shelters had been carefully researched. Structure had to be related to function, as Dennis Wood of Manchester recalls: 'In the thickly populated areas close to the city centre, brick and concrete community shelters were built, whilst a little further out where people had back gardens Anderson shelters were erected. These corrugated iron shelters were provided by local authorities but the occupants had to dig a hole and into this the walls were inserted and the roof added. Extra protection was provided by heaping the soil from the excavation on the roof and sides. Most people then planted vegetables and even a flower or two to add to the feeling of comfort as well as having the satisfaction of digging for victory.

'People really did try to make their Andersons an attractive feature. Ours, in due course, boasted two double bunks, a paraffin heater and a tiny stove on which we could boil a kettle.'

I too can remember sitting in an Anderson shelter in our garden near the docks at Barrow-in-Furness. I was four years old and learned to count during an air raid. Every explosion caused by a bomb was counted and my trembling mother told me that each bang was one of our guns shooting down a German. This was exciting and I also looked forward to older boys coming to our house to ask if they could look in our garden to collect shrapnel.

Hindpool Road, Barrow, on 9 May 1941.

Following this raid we spent several nights away from the main danger and slept in the house of my cousin Alan Hargreaves's family at Cobden Street in Dalton-in-Furness. There were 17 people there including a Salvation Army officer named Major (Miss) Brewer. She saved us all by reacting to the sound of each falling bomb by shouting 'God love us all'. It must have worked because both Alan and I are alive to recall the incident.

There has been some confusion with regard to who 'invented' the shelter because there seem to have been two Andersons involved. The construction of these cheap and easy to construct shelters was considered to be essential and even by 1938 there was a demand for a morale-boosting domestic shelter to be produced. The Home Secretary of the time was John Anderson (later Sir) and on 10th November

25

1938 he commissioned an engineer named William Paterson, who had an assistant called David Anderson, to design a cheap yet functional shelter as soon as possible. The design was delivered within a week and by the following week the first shelter was ready to be demonstrated. It seems unlikely to me that an ambitious politician would miss an opportunity to have these life-saving structures named after him. It is satisfying, however, to also recognise the man who played a major role in the design.

By February 1939 shelters were being erected in London and eventually 2,300,000 had been delivered to homes throughout the UK. People who earned less than £250 per year were given a shelter free but the more affluent had to pay £7.

What did they get for their money? There were 14 sheets of corrugated iron, which had to be bolted together to form a shell measuring 6 ft high, 4 ft 6 ins wide and 6 ft 6 ins long. A hole of at least 4 ft in depth had to be dug, into which the shelter was inserted. Many Andersons were constructed in the winter of 1940, which was one of the coldest on record. I remember my father having to use a pick and shovel to break up the ground. Many strong men earned a few extra shillings at this time digging the holes, but the old or disabled were helped by the local authorities. It was recommended that the shelter should be covered by at least 15 inches of soil and many people also followed Dennis Wood's example by making their Anderson comfortable.

There was, however, one major problem - because the Andersons were buried in the ground, flooding was almost impossible to prevent. My father, like me, was not a very handy chap and we soon flooded. Uncle Billy, a very practical chap, came to the rescue and we soon had a shelter that was cold and damp as opposed to very cold and flooded! Many people bought sawdust, which they spread into the water as it seeped in.

There is no doubt that the Anderson could provide

This posed photograph taken in Chorley in 1939 is a lighthearted look at life in an Anderson shelter, but Andersons like the one in Fog Lane, Didsbury (below), did see some action in 1940.

Inside an Anderson shelter, at Preston Museum.

protection except for a direct hit and they did save many lives. A few Andersons have been preserved in museums, one of the best examples in the North West being at Preston.

Many town and city dwellers, however, did not have gardens and were also some distance away from the large communal brick shelters. This led to the invention and production of what became known as Morrison shelters, named after Herbert Morrison, who was then the Minister of Home Security. The shelter was issued free to all who were in need and was designed for use indoors. It had a solid steel top mounted on solid legs and the structure could therefore function as a table. This was 2 ft 9 ins high and had sides composed of a very sturdy wire mesh. By the end of 1941 some 500,000 Morrison shelters were in use. These, although obviously heavy, were much more easily assembled than the Anderson. They were also much more versatile and apart from their use as a dining table they were also ideal for table tennis!

One other shelter, which was purely functional, was the Consol, which looked like a huge metal shell but was fitted with a door which could be secured from the inside. Within there was room for only one or at the most two people to shelter whilst engaged in fire watching. At the top was a very solid metal ring, which was used to carry the shelter by means of a crane onto a roof or other high vantage point. Few people know about these shelters but there are two fine examples at the entrance to the Museum of Lancashire in Preston. One of these came from the railway sidings at Kearsley near Bolton and was used by a signalman whilst on fire-watch duty. John Davies of Preston told me of his work for the police when in the 1940s he did research on mobile radio equipment. He recalled that one-man metal shelters were positioned close to the experimental radio masts near Calder Vale near Garstang.

The Consol shelter, used while fire-watching.

In contrast to these shell-like small shelters, communal shelters were designed to protect a number of people but the design was not quite so simple as is often made out. Terry Perkins of Manchester told me: 'There was a feverish spate of building brick air-raid shelters which took up half the space of the backyards of our terraced rows. With a 10-inch thick concrete roof and brick walls some 2 ft thick there was some feeling of security engendered by their presence. We were convinced that they would survive anything but a direct hit and on some nights it became the practice to sleep out in these cold dark refuges. In the outside wall, which faced out into the rear entry that ran between the rows of houses, was a 2 ft square hole with wedge-shaped removable bricks that tapered inwards. This meant that the blast would not blow them inside but push them outwards and thus not allow pieces to splinter and cause injuries inside the buildings.'

Marlene Jaques of Burnley recalls that their backyard shelter was like the one described above but they also had

Morrison shelters had lots of uses!

their own bolt hole attached to the house. This doubled as the toilet, which was a 'long drop' with a tumbler drain from the kitchen and rain overflow. 'My dad put a plank across the hole of the lavatory and bedding was put on this flat place. Timbers to support the roof were added and provided a refuge for us and also for our cats and dogs.'

Many factories built their own air-raid shelters. I spoke to Peter Hargreaves, whose family history of textiles dates back to James Hargreaves, the 18th-century inventor of the spinning jenny. James lived at Stanhill between Blackburn and Accrington and the Hargreaves family still live in the area. Here they operate the locally famous Oswaldtwistle Mills retail outlet. Part of the complex now houses a textile museum but there is an area devoted to the events of the Second World War. Peter showed me three air-raid shelters which operated during this period. One is deep underground and is used as a sales outlet for textiles, while the two purpose-built outdoor shelters now serve as classrooms for craft courses which are run regularly at the Mills. Once you know that these were once shelters it is easy to appreciate their former function.

Gerald Rawstron of Great Harwood also remembers what he described as conventional shelters, but there were others adapted to local conditions. 'We had public air-raid shelters but unlike in the big cities we never used them during an air raid, but they were marvellous play areas during the day. There were also underground shelters in Cutt Wood in Rishton. These were entered via trap doors at the top. As children we were still playing in them as late as 1948. They were eventually sealed and I suppose filled in. There is certainly no indication now that they ever existed.'

Some schools built their own shelters and in Wigan deep holes were dug and lined with concrete. Country estate owners also dug their own staff shelters. The Earl of Crawford whose estate was at Haigh Hall on the outskirts of Wigan (now a Country Park) built his own retreat. This shelter

Some schools, including this one in Wigan, had their own purpose-built shelters. This photograph taken in 1940 shows boys emerging after the all clear.

was very solid indeed and may have also secretly doubled as headquarters for a specially trained Home Guard unit. This would have been important in the event of an invasion.

Natural features such as caves were also converted into shelters, as at Liverpool and especially at Stockport. People from Manchester travelled to spend the night in the Stockport cave shelters. These have now been developed into a splendid museum telling the history of the Blitz in the Manchester area.

Some people who had the skills necessary built their own shelters, as did Betty Parton's father, who was a builder with his yard in St Helens. He strengthened the cellar of the house and reinforced the ceilings. Joyce Kershawe of Brooklands near Manchester recalls: 'My father made a shelter for us in the cellar, which consisted of sheets of corrugated iron on the ceiling supported by steel girders. However, more often than not we went into an even deeper underground shelter built in Dr Chamrett's surgery on Chester Road. This was built to house up to 200 people and had wooden forms all along the walls. At the bottom of the stairs was a small room which was used as a kitchen and people used to brew up in a big water boiler.

'If we stayed at our home shelter we had two comfortable fireside chairs plus a bundle of bedding, food and a change of clothing. Along with all this my mother carried her precious handbag containing important documents including insurance policies.'

Which brings me to one area of the conflict that has not often been studied and this is compensation for losses

Private estates often had their own air raid shelters. This one belonged to the Earl of Crawford at Haigh Hall. It may well have been secretly used by special units of the Home Guard.

incurred by the war, which were not covered by conventional insurance. Some institutions did manage to arrange some form of insurance. The little village church of St John the Evangelist at Calder Vale near Garstang, for instance, negotiated an insurance policy in the event of bombing. The bell was valued at £50, the furniture at £200 and the organ at £350.

There was a government insurance scheme to help those who lost property or their houses as a result of the Blitz, officially called 'The War Damage Act 1943 - the Private Chattels Act'. It could be backdated but the paperwork took a long time to be dealt with. Elsie Selby of 6 Boundary Lane, London SE17, had her home bombed in May 1941 and moved away to live with relatives in Bacup. She was eventually paid £35 10s 0d on 8th April 1946! The Board of Trade Insurance and Companies Department was based in Isleworth in Middlesex and must have been inundated with claims, each of which had to be checked. It is no wonder that it took time to deal with the forms and make contact with displaced persons.

Chapter 2

Women and Children at War

The Second World War substantially affected the lives of Lancashire women and their children. Some found themselves living far from home as the evacuation programme took effect, and most women worked for the war effort in some way – either conscripted into the factories, shipyards and hospitals, where they did a man's work for the duration, or voluntarily for indispensable bodies such as the Women's Voluntary Service.

The Control of Employment Orders of 1939 and 1943 directed women into engineering, shipyards, ordnance and aircraft factories, hospitals and indeed anywhere that there was a labour shortage. What was very unfair is that they were paid a lot less than men for doing the exact same job. The best that a woman could hope for was 75% of the man's rate and most had to be content with much less. In some factories the workers were on piecework and hardworking women proved their point by earning more than some of the less efficient men who worked alongside them! This even applied when men were on a higher basic rate.

Women were forced into this most essential work and the only exemptions were if they were pregnant, had children under 14 or had what was described as 'great family responsibilities'. From April 1941 women had to register for work and those between the ages of 16 and 49 were directed into designated occupations. After December 1941 women without children were subject to the National Services Act and could be conscripted into the armed services. Those already in essential jobs such as factory work, nursing or the Land Army were exempt but some girls made a special effort to join the armed services and many were successful. By 1943, 90% of single women and 80% of married women, with children over fourteen, were working.

Women were urgently needed to take the place of men called up into the Services.

Many of those women worked on the land, as members of the Women's Land Army, and their contribution is described more fully in Chapter 5. However, the munitions and aircraft factories also needed more and more female labour; the Dunkirk evacuation in 1940 had saved men but not armaments and lots of essential equipment had to be replaced very quickly. Output from every factory involved in the arms trade was increased and eleven-hour shifts and night working were needed. In September 1942 Clement Attlee, the

Women proved to be more than capable of doing a man's work. These ladies were working on a bus engine at the Hyde Road works in Manchester.

Labour leader and Deputy Prime Minister, spoke in praise of women, saying, 'The work that women are performing in munitions factories has to be seen to be believed. Precision engineering which a few years ago would have made a skilled turner's hair stand on end is now being performed with dead accuracy by girls who have had no industrial experience.'

Accidents did happen but a cloak of secrecy was wrapped over these sad events. A newspaper report of September 1943 was deliberately kept vague: 'Two women were killed and four men injured in an explosion which ripped the roof off a factory building in the North-West of England last night. Fire which followed was put out by the National Fire Service.'

There seemed to be one fundamental difference between men and women employed in the grimy atmosphere of the

37

Lancashire's mill lasses soon adapted and became engineers and armament workers.

workshop. Women were prepared to get dirty whilst working but had no intention of going home dirty. A working man coming home dirty was telling his family how hard he had worked. Women had no intention of losing part of their pride or their femininity. They used Glymiel jelly, which was said to have antiseptic properties, to keep their hands smooth, whilst at 11s 9d, plus 7d postage, many girls purchased an attractive looking boiler suit made by Barkers. Women also became much more liberated, as Alan Hargreaves, who was a teenager in the war years, remembers, 'Young women coming out of a small munitions factory near Tudor Square at Dalton-in-Furness wore their hair tied up neatly in head scarves. For the first time I saw girls wearing make up during the day and for the first time I saw women smoking openly in public.'

By the end of 1943, 57% of all factory workers were female. Strong women were employed in the docks but even the elderly and housebound were encouraged to do their bit. Some assembled at home items such as small yet intricate parts for aeroplanes and guns, and those with physical handicaps also worked efficiently on various assembly projects and were proud of doing their bit.

Many women who were not officially 'in work' actually laboured longer and harder and yet received no pay. The best example of this was the Women's Voluntary Service (WVS, later the Women's Royal Voluntary Service). This was initiated in the autumn of 1938 when the Home Secretary asked the Dowager Lady Reading to recruit women to help with the air raid precautions. By the end of 1938 there were more than 38,000 members.

As other colours had been earmarked by other women's services, the WVS chose a shade of green for their uniform. This they had to pay for themselves, which was acceptable because the women who joined were usually from the better-off middle and upper classes. As some people thought that green was unlucky, grey was also woven into the fabric and a beetroot red colour was incorporated into the jumper and hat trimming.

The first task of these ladies, whose organisation was first called the Women's Voluntary Service for Air Raid Precautions, was to supervise the evacuation programme, which began in September 1939 and is described in more detail below. In excess of 210,000 women staffed reception

WVS ladies ready to serve tea for those passing through Carnforth in 1942.

areas and others screened potential foster homes. About 400 WVS nurseries were established for the under fives in what were described as 'safe' areas.

Early in 1941, eighteen Queen's Messenger Convoys funded from the USA were put into commission, each consisting of twelve mobile canteens and emergency water supplies. Each was staffed by women volunteers who were prepared to be rushed into disaster areas. Having one large water tank, two food storage units, three mobile canteens, two equipment lorries with army field kitchens and four motorcycles, each unit was able to provide up to 10,000 emergency meals per day.

During the bombing, the WVS ran Incident Enquiry Points, organised sheltered welfare and rest centres whilst giving comfort both material and physical to those made homeless. Some 1,750 of the WVS centres were active during the war and a Roll of Honour set up at Westminster Abbey records the 241 ladies who were killed as a direct result of enemy action.

I heard of a vicar's wife involved in classifying evacuees, who she labelled C, D and VD. This alarmed many people until they translated her shorthand as Clean, Dirty and Very Dirty! The war did much to broaden the horizons of these middle class ladies!

Mrs Rose Davis of Oswaldtwistle remembers these times very well and she has been helped by reference to her diaries, which she has kept since 1926: 'We were all given lessons in first aid and we were detailed in pairs. Some of my friends and relatives were doctors and there were ladies who were used to seeing injuries so I hoped to pair up with one of them who could help me if the time came. Our group also helped to wrap bandages, which were usually cut from old sheets. Many cotton mills were closed because of a shortage of imports but there were odd bits of what we called shed cotton lying about which we recycled. Make Do and Mend meant just that. Some of today's so-called experts on recycling need to take notice of what we got up to in the war. Almost everything was recycled including paper, clothes, rubber, aluminium, pots and pans, iron railings and even old bones that were collected and made into glue. Collection points were organised mainly by the WVS.'

During these times everybody had to get used to fictional characters such as 'Detective Inspector Waste' and 'Superintendent Salvage' which children learned to love. The bones not only made glue for aircraft construction but also glycerine, which was the base for some explosives. Tins and other metals were sometimes capable of being recycled for use in tanks and aircraft. These days we think that it is progress to have separate containers for metal, paper and rags but in the 1940s this separation was taken for granted and children often eagerly took the lead by following these comical characters.

The WVS ladies arranged meetings to teach housewives

how to 'Make Do and Mend', and a poster campaign was organised to publicise this scheme and also to fight 'the Squander Bug'.

Children were also looked after and there was a well organised scheme to renovate and recycle toys for Christmas. Once this was up and running families could discuss how to organise birthday celebrations for those too young to realise what had gone on in peacetime.

Amusement is one thing, but the good health of children was obviously of vital importance with special emphasis being placed upon the provision of Vitamin C. Citrus fruits, especially oranges, were not available during the war and a substitute had to be found. Rosehip syrup was found to be the answer but the problem was how to collect the volume of rosehips required. Children from rural areas could collect the fruit but this had to be carefully organised. Once again the WVS was brought into action and used the schools as collection points. I remember this scheme very well as a seven year old in 1943. We were asked to collect rosehips and take them to school. They were weighed and for each pound we were given a new shiny eight-sided 3d piece. I'm sure that I learned to be a naturalist at this time because growing on our sand dunes at Askam-in-Furness was the Burnet rose. This was even more prickly than the dog rose but produced higher doses of Vitamin C. The black hips were valued at 4d per pound!

Another essential job carried out by the WVS was to organise courses on how to make the best use of rations. Some members were specially trained to be what became known as 'Food Leaders'. They not only advised on recipes but also gave advice on how to prepare meals when gas and electricity supplies were disrupted following air raids. Those who could drive were given a strictly controlled petrol allowance to deliver leaflets. One was entitled 'Information on Bed Wetting' for those taking in evacuees.

This relates to the WVS's main function and it is to this

emotive subject that I now turn. The evacuee programme has dominated the story of civilian life during the Second World War and it is right that it should do so.

In 1938 plans were made in the event of war to evacuate not only children, but also pregnant women, invalids, blind people and also the elderly. As it happened, it was mainly children who were affected. In the so-called phoney war of 1939/1940, when the belligerents seemed to pause for breath, some children were sent away only to be brought home again. Off they went again when the war started in earnest. If we look at vulnerable children today,

DON'T *do it,*
Mother—

LEAVE THE CHILDREN WHERE THEY ARE

ISSUED BY THE MINISTRY OF HEALTH

Evacuation was voluntary but emotional pressure was put on parents to send their children away from the cities.

this coming and going in the war period must have been, to say the least, traumatic.

In the first four days of September 1939, 1,500,000 parents took up the offer to have their children evacuated (which was purely voluntary) to so-called safer areas. The list of what evacuee children were to pack for their journey was compiled by well-meaning but obviously middle-class ladies. Many parents from the so-called 'slum areas' would never have owned all such 'essential' items. For example:

Boys: 1 vest, 1 pair of pants, 1 pair of trousers, 2 pairs of socks, handkerchiefs and 1 pullover or jersey.

Girls: 1 vest, 1 pair of knickers, 1 petticoat, 2 pairs of stockings, handkerchiefs, 1 slip, 1 blouse, 1 cardigan.

Both sexes: An overcoat or mackintosh, a comb, towel,

Children waiting to be picked up after their journey.

facecloth, toothbrush, boots or shoes, plimsolls. Each child had to carry a gas mask in its case and a packed meal. This was to consist of sandwiches, packets of nuts and seedless raisins, dry biscuits, barley sugar but not 'proper' sugar, plus an apple and an orange.

Obviously at this stage rationing had not begun to bite but these lists were simply not realistic for poor families.

These poor mites were then packed off in special trains not knowing where they were going. Some had never been much further than their own back street. Even worse was to come as the Reception Centres were reached and the selection process began, which in retrospect has been compared to a slave auction. In other places a WVS billeting officer would put children in her car and tour the area asking if householders would take them in.

Mrs Jean Turner, who now lives in Burnley, has vivid memories of this time in her life: 'I was about four years old and living in Manchester. I vaguely remember the noise of the bombs and seeing the searchlights trying to follow the planes. I also remember being put into a cot in the hospital with other children. We were all piled together and there was a nurse running very fast with us down a corridor to an underground shelter. We thought it was great fun at the time.

'My next memory is being put on a train with lots of other children; there was lots of crying not by us children but in our case by our mum. She was telling my elder sister who was six to look after me. She was telling us not to be split up. We then set off on the train both wearing ID bracelets with our name on. Everyone was singing *John Brown's Body*.

'Then I remember being in a school hall and children began to go away with adults. There were then only a few adults left and I realised that they were talking about my sister Mary and me. The conversation centred around a reluctance to take both of us. Eventually a lady agreed to have us and I now know that we were among the lucky ones. So began the next two very happy years. Two little urchins from the poor area of Manchester and our Dad had joined up as a regular soldier just to get a job. At our foster home we were taught lovely manners, disciplined behaviour and how to do things for ourselves. Auntie and Uncle had two grown up children of their own. Margaret was a schoolteacher at St John's in Darwen and Tom worked for Boots the Chemists. We lived in Greenway Street and went to St Cuthbert's School. Sometimes Auntie would let us have a lift on the milkman's horse and cart but usually we walked, but school was not very far away.

'We were well fed and beautifully clothed and our "Auntie and Uncle" must have spent a lot of time and money on our upbringing. I think people got money for having refugees but they spent much more than they received. We were shown

*Evacuees David and Michael Thomson were taken for a day trip to Morecambe
by their host, Mrs Robinson of Balderstone, near Blackburn.*

how to do things for ourselves. If Mary wet the bed she was
in trouble and Auntie's cure was to rub her nose in it. This
helped me not to do it.

'We had to sit each evening with our fingers on our lips
to listen to the six o'clock news on the wireless. Once this
was over we were allowed to get a big cardboard box from
under the settee and play with our toys, which had once
belonged to Tom and Margaret, but they were all new to us.
After this we could choose whose knee to sit on to say our
prayers. When I hear the stories of other refugees I realise
now just how lucky we were.'

Another lucky couple of youngsters were David and
Michael Thomson. They were billeted with Mrs Robinson
of Balderstone, near Blackburn. She even managed to take
the brothers to Morecambe on a day trip!

Parents had to make up their minds whether or not to

send their children away, as evacuation was not compulsory. Rick Brent was only six when war began in 1939 but he has vivid memories of the 1940 Blitz in Manchester: 'Food supplies were beginning to get short, and rationing was soon introduced. I stayed at home with my mother until the Christmas Blitz of 1940. The raids became incessant, every night, night after night. I remember having to go down our cellar at home with my mother and sister during raids, and sit on the bottom step, listening to the exploding bombs and the whistling noises as they descended on Manchester. On one particular day, the raid started at 6 pm, and carried on until 5 am next morning. One bomb whistled so loud, that my mother thought that this was it! It shattered our windows, and the dust and plaster fell onto our heads and covered the cellar floor. I can still see my mother praying out loud each time a bomb whistled close by. The house next door but one was completely demolished. Only a very small baby was pulled out alive. The air was full of smoke, and fires were raging in all directions. The street was covered with hosepipes and I remember seeing people wandering aimlessly about, crying in total desperation.

'That was enough for my mother! She had me evacuated two days later. I was put into the back of a van and ended up in a place called Timperley. There were eight children in the van. We stopped just off Deansgate Lane, and several people were waiting to take a child. All the children were taken except me, and I stood there in the back of the van petrified, and crying my eyes out. I thought nobody wanted me. I was very small and puny, and my glasses had that sticky plaster over one of the lenses - but someone took pity on me, and I joined their family.

'They were the Normans of Hall Avenue, and they had a son, aged ten, named Peter, who had laid out a Hornby train set on the living room floor to take my mind off everything. I had a bedroom with lots of books, something I'd never had before. There was a bathroom – again, something I had never seen with hot and cold running water, and an inside loo. Cor! It was Buckingham Palace – even a garden at the rear with green grass and trees! But even with all this, I still cried for two or three days. I was there for three years, and it became a very happy time for me. I went to Navigation Road school on the electric train, it was all a far cry from my humble Victorian terrace in Hulme. My parents moved from Hulme to Wythenshaw in 1943, where I rejoined them at the age of ten. My childhood as an evacuee was an admirable experience that I will never forget. I have recently discovered that the boy Peter, who I befriended over 60 years ago, is now 74 and lives in West Yorkshire. Yes, being an evacuee was something that certainly changed my whole outlook on life. It was an awe-inspiring adventure.'

Whenever we think of children growing up during the Second World War we should also give some thought to their teachers. Many men were called up but some very experienced staff were too old to be drafted into the armed forces.

The best teachers set about making life exciting for those they taught. None was more able or more vociferous than Sam Hanna, who taught at Abel Street School in Burnley. Sam was a born communicator but also a pioneer in the art of film making. In later years Sam's films about old crafts, but especially of events during the war, have been preserved for posterity. Sam, however, never lost touch with his lads, and he made woodworking a thrill. During the war his pupils made models of tanks and Spitfires and I still treasure the photograph he gave me of a model that his pupils had made.

After we were bombed out of Barrow we moved to Askam-in-Furness. In the pale-coloured stone infants' school one of our teachers was Mrs Shaw. Almost in defiance of the then traditional methods of teaching she devoted the whole of Friday afternoon to Nature Study. Whenever possible this was done outside. Wet days were spent writing up and we were given a special little notebook to write down the names of the flowers that we found. She even gave us the Latin names because we were in her top class and about to move on to the 'big school'. I am certain that my working life as an ecologist travelling the world and keeping a detailed diary for more than 50 years was due to the influence of Mrs Shaw.

All round the school were posters pointing out that the Germans were a nasty lot and spent all of their time disguising bombs or gas grenades to look like toys. This

Sam Hanna's wonderful inspiration allowed his Burnley pupils to conquer their fear of war through play. They also learned woodworking skills.

was worrying but at the same time exciting. There was a section of our local beach which was not being used by the military, and here Mrs Shaw delighted us by pointing out that a living crab, a starfish or a sea anemone was hardly likely to explode. I remember her wise words to this day: 'Don't touch anything you don't understand,' she told us.

She gave us pencils and paper on which we were allowed to draw the creatures we found. We each had our own pencil and, because supplies were short in wartime, you had to show that one was worn out before you were issued with another. Marlene Jaques recalls handing in her remnant of a worn pencil, when she was accused of biting it down and was smacked!

The paper Mrs Shaw gave us had to be used on both sides and we were asked to write neatly but keep the letters small. My handwriting is still small, more than 60 years later, and I'm sure that my wartime experience is the reason. I was recognised as the best writer in the class but also regarded as the worst artist by many a mile. My friend George Hughes was a good drawer but not a neat writer. We worked together and as our nature notes were not being marked, Mrs Shaw turned a blind eye to our partnership.

Some children, however, honed their artistic talents to perfection during the war. There were so few options on offer in those days that I'm sure the attention span of the children was far greater. Toys were played with longer and hobbies were given more time, as were physical activities. Art was a wonderful distraction.

Few people realise that the famous Pendelfin series of ceramics evolved during the war. If ever a Lancashire lass had a rare and precocious talent it was Jean Walmsley, who was born in the Tim Bobbin pub on Padiham Road in Burnley. She was already selling her paintings whilst attending Ightenhill school and the turning point in her life came in 1939 when she was turned down by the Royal Navy and drafted into industry. She was set to work on army

Jean Walmsley, seen here on the left in the 1950s, overseeing her wartime nursery designs for wallpaper being developed into world famous ceramics.

uniforms and items of leather for the military. Her artistic talents also took the form of designing presents for visiting dignitaries and this work eventually led to the establishment of Pendelfin, which involved the skilled use of ceramics. In 1943 she was released from her job in textiles because of a commission to design wall murals to brighten up the bleak and colourless walls of children's nurseries. These murals were actually commissioned by the Canadian Red Cross and produced as a gift to the children of Britain. The designs were later adapted and improved upon as the Pendelfin Ceramics factory evolved, which, until early 2006, was based at an old mill on Cameron Street in Burnley.

All this relates to 'resident' children, if that is the right expression – those who received their education and then went home at night to eat with their parents. I have, however, also been discussing the lives of those poor mites who were removed from home at a vulnerable age and had to adapt to living with strangers.

Do we have an individual who could clearly put into words the story of the evacuee? Indeed we do, and Jack Rosenthal, who died in 2004, achieved fame and fortune by means of his pen. Jack was born in Manchester and his Jewish father worked in the clothing trade. Jack was evacuated to Colne, where he made lasting friends, and went off to Sheffield University. After this he began to write plays and his big break came when he devised and wrote the first episodes of *Coronation Street*. Later he wrote a famous and very accurate dramatisation about evacuees, which he admitted

Refugees were to be found in many Lancashire towns. In 1938, for example, these Czechoslovak Jewish lads were brought from Sudetenland, away from the Germans, to be made welcome in Burnley.

was largely, if not totally, autobiographical. This was broadcast in 1975 and his Colne experiences were adapted to fit into the scenario of wartime Blackpool. The fear of war almost certainly meant more to the Jewish chi'dren evacuated from London to Lancashire. Some of the older children remembered coming as refugees from the tyranny of the Nazis, and most would have some experience of the persecution of their race. No wonder youngsters like Jack felt insecure as war loomed.

Jack Rosenthal's story, and that of Mrs Jean Turner described above, show the happy side of the life of evacuees but not all children were so well looked after. Joyce Kilshaw of Brooklands near Manchester recalls, 'I was nine years old when I was evacuated just before the outbreak of war. We were all taken to Victoria station in Manchester and I remember looking at the huge map on the wall and wondering where we would end up. We eventually arrived at Great Harwood. Every child was issued with a rucksack and we were given two bars of chocolate. Sadly we did not eat them because we were too worried, but our "new parents" took them off us on arrival and I never saw them again. The homesickness was terrible and after six weeks we were contemplating running away and following the railway tracks back home. Fortunately my mother came to visit us and she arranged to bring us back home.'

Some children became more travelled than their parents. Terry Perkins was a streetwise kid in Manchester and evacuation gave him the opportunity to explore Lancashire: 'When Manchester looked like receiving a beating we three boys aged ten, eight and six were sent to the Silesian College in Pott Shrigley near Macclesfield. Our mother and young sister were billeted with a Mrs Johnson in Poynton, about three miles away. She lived in a bungalow with French windows at the rear, which overlooked a huge rose bed and the smell was lovely. Mrs Johnson had a maid and two teenage sons who, were at boarding school. When they came home for the holidays they played cricket in a field behind the garden. Dressed in cream flannel trousers and blazers adorned with badges, they were in a different world as far as we were concerned but, when we visited my mum, we were allowed to join in.

The priests' training seminary where we evacuees were placed was hardly well equipped to look after a crowd of Manchester kids dropping suddenly into their cloistered existence. The college had at one time been a private residence and was beautifully situated with an ornamental lake teeming with fish. Two boats in the shape of swans were a delight to us. They tended to leak and part of the fun was to bale them out before they sank. The food was very basic but we never went hungry. We used to sit at long refectory tables waiting patiently for the priest in charge to say grace. We all thought that we were young monks in training.

'We returned to Manchester for a while but the bombing became even more of a problem and off we went on our travels for a second time. After a parachute mine attack we reported to our school in Holt Town as usual and were told at assembly to go home immediately and collect our clothing and gas masks and to report back at one o'clock. Off we went in a fleet of double-decker buses. I was to spend more than three years as an evacuee, staying at Wilpshire near Blackburn for six months and for the rest of the time between Newton and Slaidburn in the Trough of Bowland.

'On arrival in Wilpshire we were taken to the church hall and we all sat in family clusters on the floor. Shortly, groups of people came into the room and began to decide which ones to take. Eventually my younger brother and I were chosen to go with a portly and amiable cigar-smoking man and his wife, who began by looking very, very closely at us. We were bundled into his Vauxhall car and soon arrived at a large detached house.

'Some of the young evacuees, including my brother, got so homesick that they had to go home but others like me took to this life like a duck to water. At the age of eleven my life had changed forever and the sounds and sights of the countryside meant everything to me. The Trough of Bowland still draws me back all these years later.'

It is no wonder that Terry Perkins became a naturalist, a historian and now Chairman of the Manchester and High Peak Ramblers' Association. This ex-refugee had his future way of life forged by his wartime experiences.

Many families were evacuated by travelling to kind relatives living in safer areas. Theresa Howard, who is 74 and now lives in Little Mountain, Australia, recalls her 'kind Uncle John', who lived in the Mill Hill area of Blackburn: 'It was after the heavy air raids in Liverpool in May 1941 that Uncle John brought my mother, sisters and I to stay with his wife and daughter Emma. It was like another world to get away from our war-torn area and to me Uncle John was

Theresa Howard photographed with her mother by her uncle, John Howard of Mill Hill in Blackburn. Her kind uncle gave them a home away from the Liverpool bombing in 1940.

Father Christmas visiting the children of Blackpool in 1942.

the kindest man I had ever known. I will never forget what he said to me when we had first arrived in Mill Hill: "Wud thee like thy likeness took, lass?" With that he pointed his Box Brownie and took our photograph. He also gave the children a bar of chocolate and there was a bunch of flowers for my mum. I soon settled in at the school called St Peter's In Chains and we were all safer and happier whilst in Blackburn. Our teachers were friendly too and they played their part in keeping children happy during the war.'

It can also be said that teaching and learning changed as a result of the war. The role of women in teaching became more appreciated at this time, with the recognition that they could actually teach senior boys and take an active part in scientific subjects and mathematics. Many influential parents whose children were evacuated had closed minds and did not trust 'rural women teachers'. In fact, the standard of teaching of the 'three Rs' was almost certainly higher in country districts than was the case in towns and cities. The discipline was certainly better. Married women teachers also became more acceptable and this led directly to a more rounded education for children. Teaching in the open air also became acceptable and led to lots of creative writing, while the standards of writing, spelling and grammar were not compromised in any way. Maths was also more easily taught by reference to the weights, measures and costings imposed by rationing. The portions did not remain constant but varied in response to supply and demand.

Not all the relations between evacuees and their hosts went so smoothly, as Mrs Rose Davies recalls: 'Most of the little mites were fine but some were crafty little beggars and had to be taught not to be light fingered, but the adults did not help. The fathers often came at weekends but seemed not to bother much with their kids. It was only when they had gone home that local folk began to miss chickens and eggs.'

What the evacuee system did was to free up large numbers of women who could contribute to the war effort. This was more obvious in the big cities such as Manchester

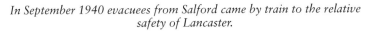

In September 1940 evacuees from Salford came by train to the relative safety of Lancaster.

and Liverpool but all the smaller towns had to change. Lancaster, for example, with its traditionally up-market factories had to adapt quickly. There were very few surplus men, and women were eager, willing and very able to fill the gap. Storeys, for example, adapted from the manufacture of oilcloth to making gas capes, blackout fabric and waterproof materials. As production targets were continually being raised, more and more women answered the call. The Standfast Company specialised in making tropical uniforms, bullet-proof vests, tents and camouflage nets. Even the famous furniture firm of Waring and Gillow had to bow to the demands of the war effort and women along with men brought back from retirement produced utility furniture, most of which

A mum and daughter in typical 1940s clothes, photographed at a railway 1940s weekend at the Embsay Steam Railway, near Skipton.

went to victims who had lost everything in the blitz.

The Royal Army Pay Corps was also based at Lancaster and there was a huge demand for female civilian clerks. No doubt Lancaster was considered to be relatively safe and that is probably why 4,000 evacuees were poured into the city during one week of 1940. This put a lot of pressure on schools and, as in many places, children were taught in shifts with their teachers often coming with them. It is easy to imagine the pressure, too, that was put onto railways and buses at this time, when transport also had to meet the needs of the armed services and of industry.

Chapter 3

Is Your Journey Really Necessary?

You wonder why we make a fuss
If George decides to take a bus,
But look again and you will see
That George ain't all that George should be.

He's only got a step to go,
A couple of hundred yards or so,
While others further down the queue
Have far to go and lots to do.

When George gets on we often find
That other folk get left behind.
He pays his fare and rides the stage
And off he hops to see the rage.
And seeing this gives George a jog,
'Perhaps I'm just a Transport Hog?'

Posters soon appeared appealing to travellers to consider whether they really needed to make a journey.

As the war began in 1939, railway stations displayed colourful posters that asked all travellers to consider: 'Is Your Journey Really Necessary?' The pressure placed upon rail, road and canal in the north-west of England as Britain fought against invasion in the years that followed meant the transport system almost, but thankfully not quite, ground to a halt.

Rail

During the war the rail network had to handle a greater volume of, and at times much heavier, traffic than in peacetime; trains had to be blacked out, bomb damage had to be repaired and loads prioritised according to need. Old engines had to be put back into service and more and more locomotives had to be built. Worn out track had to be replaced or repaired at great speed.

At that time there were four main regionalised railways, each with their own types of locomotives, marshalling yards and repair depots. In Lancashire the LMS (London, Midland and Scottish) was the provider but during the war all the companies had to work together, and after the war nationalisation was accomplished more smoothly than would otherwise have been the case. In fact, a Railway Executive Committee was set up just before September 1939 and this virtually nationalised the whole system. Passenger services were stripped down to a minimum whilst sleeping units and restaurant cars were taken out of service. Each locomotive had to pull more and more coaches or trucks and speed was reduced accordingly.

There were many crew restrictions, including an order that they were not to take cover during air attacks. It was considered that a moving train was much less vulnerable than one that remained stationary. Each lamp on the engine was masked, crews had to drive almost blind and blackout curtains covered the cab so that the boiler fires could not be seen from the air when the fireman was stoking up. Shifts were long and unpredictable and some men were on the footplate for more than 20 hours at a time. Meals were often cooked on a shovel heated in the boiler. In summer conditions could be unbearable on humid nights as heat was trapped under the blackout tarpaulin.

To the railwaymen the evacuee programme was known as 'Operation Pied Piper' and there was not a single fatal accident despite the huge numbers involved. The Dunkirk evacuation in May/June 1940 – Operation Dynamo – meant injured soldiers were carried to hospitals all over the country from the south coast, including many areas around north-western England. Some 620 trains carried 300,000 men to hundreds of locations and this put a huge strain upon locomotives, rolling stock and personnel. The answer was, as always – send for the women! By 1943, 105,000 women were employed on the railways doing all jobs except those of driver and fireman. It would normally have involved long periods of training for these jobs and the one thing that was not available was time. The Luftwaffe recognised the importance of railways and their records show that they mounted 9,000 raids specifically against the system. Amazingly, they destroyed only eight engines in that time.

The railway system was under pressure all through the war but, with the lead up to D-Day, the American saying: 'You ain't seen nothin' yet' was prophetic! The armament and munitions factories were working at full capacity and all this material had to be transported to where it was needed, and the only way of doing this, at least initially, was via the railway. Some 24,000 special trains were required and each had to be carefully timetabled. The railway planners and workers have not received the credit they deserve as they flogged the often antiquated system almost to death. Locomotives did wear out and had to be repaired or scrapped and replaced.

So great was the demand for steam engines that the Ministry of Defence took over the construction yards, including the well-named Vulcan factory at Newton-le-Willows, which literally worked at full steam. Under licence the factory constructed many of the 935 locomotives of the Austerity Class 2-8-0 during 1944, intended for use in Europe following the invasion, which was eventually and in great secrecy focused on Normandy. By 1942 the London, Midland and Scottish had a number of 8F freight locomotives in production but in 1944 there was a redesign and a change of name to the 2-10-0 class; in all 150 were built, of which 25 were eventually operated by British Railways, but by 1961 all were out of service. In contrast the 2-8-0 class proved to be a much more successful design and 733 were eventually transferred to British Railways. By 1967, however, all these engines had been taken out of service.

The Vulcan factory was finally closed in 2003 but by this time it was producing only marine diesel engines. The works had 4,000 employees in 1943 and, in addition to locomotives, produced 250 light tanks, 600 Matilda tanks, 10,000 large parts for torpedoes plus 40,000 smaller torpedo parts, and 1,700 machine gun mountings. Lily Jackson, née Langtree, who worked at Vulcan, recalls: 'I hated my name, which was the subject of lots of jokes on the shop floor where I was helping to assemble machine gun parts. I was glad

The Vulcan crest.

A Light Tank (Mark 6) constructed at Vulcan.
(Via George Forty, Bovington Tank Museum)

when Ted Jackson asked me to marry him in 1942 when we were both working hard at Vulcan and making good money. Better, I thought, to be an unknown Jackson than a famous Langtree.'

There was also an experimental aspect to Vulcan: from the 1930s the company had been working in conjunction with the Frich's Company in Denmark to develop diesel locomotives. This arrangement ended in 1940 when the Germans swept into Denmark. The Nazis had a research programme of their own but the Danish boffins escaped to England and brought their diesel plans with them to Vulcan.

Horwich was also a huge railway centre and its history these days has wrongly been interwoven with that of Bolton. Part of the old locomotive works has now been developed as part of the Reebok Stadium complex of Bolton Wanderers Football Club.

Horwich was once a town of spinners and weavers, first of wool and then of cotton. In 1777 the Ridgeway family set up a huge bleach works and built a large number of houses for their workers. The year 1884, however, was the most important in the history of Horwich, when the Lancashire and Yorkshire Railway Company built what became a world famous locomotive factory. The company constructed a model complex of works, hospital, school, shops, churches and houses. By 1900 the works employed 13,000 people.

During both the First and Second World Wars, Horwich built locomotives but, as at Vulcan, additional workshops were built and tanks were also constructed. As usual labour was at a premium because nearby there were coalmines and pipe and clay works requiring tough men. Women came to the rescue and at its peak 5,000 were employed at the

The 0-6-0 medium sized goods locomotives did sterling work during the war and some were built at Horwich.

Rosegrove, near Burnley, was a vital marshalling yard during the war.

locomotive works. The works only ceased production in 1983 but at that time production was concentrated upon diesel traction.

Lancashire during the war was a huge arsenal but production targets are useless without having the means to transport the product. This amount of movement required organisation and huge marshalling yards. The two most important in the North-West were at Rosegrove near Burnley and at Carnforth.

Rosegrove was a marshalling and coaling yard with a huge servicing area for steam locomotives, which closed only during the Beeching cuts of the 1960s. During the war it was the most vital link between the factories of Lancashire and Yorkshire and the docks of Liverpool and Manchester.

Keith Emmett told me that as a child he was taken by his grandfather to watch the trains: 'I can clearly remember lots of steam sounds and sights with wagons loaded up with guns and especially tanks which he told me were made at factories near Leeds. This led to my lifelong interest in trains.' Now in retirement Keith is one of the volunteers helping to run the Embsay and Bolton Abbey Steam Railway near Skipton.

Ron Ormerod of Brierfield, near Nelson, also has memories of how busy the Rosegrove depot was: 'I used to watch the engines firing-up ready for the next phase of the journey. The sheds were busy day and night with folks beavering away to keep the often ancient locomotives running. Even the rolling stock was, to say the least, well used and had to be repaired almost literally on the run. I can still remember the smell of steam, wet coal and lubricating oil. There is one thing, which was as important as the engine sheds, and which I don't think many people know about. This was the lamp room and was situated some distance from the main area obviously because of the huge volumes of oil which had to be kept in stock. All steam locomotives had to carry identification lamps to tell people what type of train it was and the nature of its cargo. The colour codes were kept

Carnforth Station has been transformed into a museum.

secret to confuse enemy spies. The lamps were kept as dim as possible and their beams directed downwards so as not to be a target for bombers.'

Carnforth station was one of the busiest in Britain, as it was a vital coaling and repair depot situated between Scotland and the South of England. The Rosegrove complex has long gone and the same can be said for Carnforth, but thankfully there is now the excellent museum and information centre to celebrate its wartime role. The station and parts of the town were used as the setting for the film *Brief Encounter*, shot in 1945. The refreshment room has been restored as in the film and a trust called 'The Friends of Carnforth Station' has turned the waiting room into a museum with wartime photographs lining the walls. There is a bookshop and a sweet shop selling traditional brands, some of which have brought back mouth-watering memories for those who had to endure rationing.

Some railways operated outside the main network. Albert Jepson was a Liverpool docker during the war and he rang me up with a question: 'Did you know about the Dockers' Umbrella? What a tourist attraction it would now be if they hadn't dismantled it in 1956. It survived the bloody war but not the planners, who said it was costing too much to maintain. The 'Umbrella' was our name for the overhead railway which opened in 1893. It was the first overhead railway in the world which was provided with automatic signalling. The cars were bumpy to say the least but you got wonderful views all over the docks and I travelled along it one May morning in 1941 and saw the damage the Luftwaffe had done overnight to our place of work. Don't let anybody tell you that working folk weren't at the forefront of that war. We were at the sharp end. I can still remember the names of all the stations even if I can't spell them. That's up to you to check up but they were Seaforth Sands, Gladstone, Alexandra, Brocklebank, Canada, Huskisson, Nelson, Clarence, Princes, Pier Head, James Street, Canning, Wapping, Brunswick, Toxteth, Herculaneum and Dingle. Dingle station building still exists and at Wapping Dock some of the old stanchions can still be seen. Liverpool Museum has one of the cars on display. I still look at this with a tear in my eye when I think that very little effort was made to preserve this Liverpool landmark. It was around seven miles in length and with Liverpool being a City of Culture for 2008 what a spectacle the Umbrella would have been. I'm 93 now and I will have snuffed it by then but somebody told me that, at the end of the First World War, 20 million passengers used this line. Don't let anybody lose this memory, lad – you write it down!'

Albert died in April 2005, but not before I told him that I had written it down.

The Dockers' Umbrella – the Liverpool Overhead Railway - in the 1940s.

Piccadilly, Manchester in 1940. Trolley buses and trams can be seen and to the right are the communal air raid shelters.

Road Transport

These days almost every family has at least one car and all efforts to persuade more and more people to use public transport seem to be doomed to failure. In the 1930s, however, very few people had cars but most workers lived within a short distance of their employment, and there were more regular tram, bus and train services than is the case today.

Lancashire made its own public transport vehicles, as already described at Vulcan and Horwich. There was also a huge tram factory run by the English Electric Company based at Strand Road in Preston. This was adapted to produce aircraft early in the war. Trams were being phased out at this time anyway but Leyland Buses and commercial vehicles were already world famous. The history of the development of bus and truck manufacture is graphically told in the Commercial Transport Museum based in the town of Leyland. Apart from buses, there is a collection of fire engines and the museum has an exhibit dealing with the work of firemen during the Blitz. There is another splendid transport museum in the Cheetham Hill area of Manchester which has a fine collection of buses in use during the war period.

In 2003, just before he died at the age of 95, I spoke to John Crossley who told me: 'It was not just big companies which produced public transport vehicles during the war. I worked for the Crossley Company in Manchester from the 1930s until it closed just after the war. Despite my name I

A 1938 Crossley trolley bus in service in the Manchester area.

A trolley bus in for repair after an air raid in Manchester in 1941.

had nothing to do with the bosses of the company although a lot of my mates thought I was there to keep an eye on them. Apart from cars we also made trolley buses and "normal" double-deckers. We were kept busy throughout the war repairing vehicles damaged by bombing and also just keeping old vehicles going. Many is the time I came to work in a morning and set to work on the wreck of a vehicle. I felt really sorry for the crews who had to operate them.'

The idea that bus drivers had an easy time in the war has to be dispelled. Trying to drive a bus in the dark with the blackout restrictions must have been a nightmare. At least train drivers and tram drivers could follow the tracks! Buses had their headlights shielded and their bumpers painted white. Blinds were fitted to windows but interior lights were dimmed and windows were covered in tape to prevent the splintering of glass.

In winter the situation became even more difficult for those who had to keep the transport system running. Everyone burned coal and, when smog was in the air, visibility was almost zero. The winters of 1940 and 1941 were much colder than average and heavy drifts of snow were almost a daily occurrence. With wartime targets to be met, the transport system had to be kept open. Obviously more people were working in Lancashire than during the depression of the 1930s and operatives were travelling further to reach some of the new armament factories. This demand meant bringing old vehicles back into service with all the problems associated with them. Men who had worked on these old vehicles were also brought back from retirement, but still labour was short. Willing women were brought in and trained on the workbench to be bus mechanics, and Manchester had a very willing team of lasses working hard in the bus service areas.

During this period each bus had a driver and a conductor and the former was a male-dominated occupation. We should remember, however, that these huge vehicles did not have power steering and turning the wheels did require considerable physical effort. As for conductors, with men being called up for the armed services the solution was obvious and urgent - the day of the female 'clippie' had arrived. Drivers would be men and conductors would be women.

John and Amy Mahon both operated buses in Burnley but despite the urgent demands of the war some draconian rules were not relaxed. For example, a man and his wife could not operate a variable bus shift together, which made life difficult as they tried to co-ordinate shifts, especially when schedules were altered at the last minute.

John told me that there were days of fog and blinding snow when he could hardly see a thing and it was even worse for the clippie because she often had to walk in front of the bus to guide the driver. 'I remember having a blazing row with an ARP chap. It was foggy and I gave my clippie a torch. She shone this at me and I followed the beam. Suddenly the warden loomed up out of the thick fog and peered at the beam from three feet away and shouted, "Put that light out, put that light out." We all burst out laughing and it kept the passengers amused for the rest of the slow trip!'

Annie Howarth was a clippie in Burnley and she also remembers: 'There were days of snow when I looked like Scott of the Antarctic but we were proud of doing a man's job as good if not better than a man. I was once voted the most glamorous clippie and there's nowt like a dose of glamour to keep the press happy. How you could look sexy in a clippie's

Clippies photographed at the Burnley depot in 1944.

Annie Howarth, Burnley's glamorous clippie in 1941

uniform beats me but I let them take my photograph. I was more proud of the group photograph which showed lots of us clippies all spruced up in our best.'

There was nothing glamorous about bus travel during the war. Because of fuel shortages, the hours during which buses could operate were restricted mainly to peak working times. They were therefore crowded and queues were controlled by the erection of barriers. The buses themselves were bursting at the seams and the phrase 'standing room only' was stretched to often unbelievable limits. This gave the conductors a real problem in trying to collect fares and some clippies were harshly disciplined for allowing passengers to alight without paying. This led to driver-only operated vehicles after the war where passengers paid on entry. It would have been far too time consuming in those days for this to be practicable and in many

77

*A single-decker bus adapted for the use of gas as a fuel, at Barden Lane,
Burnley in 1941.*

cases the vehicles of this time were constructed to ensure
that the driver operated from his cab in total isolation. He
communicated with his clippie by means of bells. At Barrow-
in-Furness an experiment was conducted in May 1944 by the
provision of what were called conscience boxes. I remember
as an eight year old taking great pride in using one of these
boxes on a 'big blue bus' which smelled of paint, but I don't
think the boxes were a great success.

The fuel shortages led to all sorts of experiments being
carried out to find alternative fuels. Keith Emmett told me
about the Burnley gas bags: 'To save fuel, some of Burnley's
single-deckers were fitted with gas bags which were filled

with town gas. They were placed on the roof and pipes led down to the engine. On Barden Lane a gas station was adapted from a gas lamp and this allowed the bus bag to be filled by a man on duty to do this. The bus ran from Burnley to Nelson via Reedley Halt but this gas service was not very safe or efficient and was replaced soon after the war.'

Ron Ormerod also remembers these gas-bag buses and pointed out to me that gas was not a problem because Burnley area at that time was surrounded by coal mines and there were lots of gasometers providing town gas. He also made the point that coke was available as a by-product following the production of gas. During the cold winters of the war period, women and children used to visit the gas works to buy coke. I remember such a visit to the Barrow gasworks. On the outward journey I was allowed to ride in the pram but my space was occupied by a bag of coke on the return journey and I had to walk in the freezing cold.

Even cars were adapted to run on gas and Manchester developed a mobile gas production unit to supply these vehicles.

A gas-powered car, 1941.

Canals

Ron Ormerod also told me that some of the coal mines around Burnley were close to the canal and situated there for obvious reasons. In the modern context of travel we look upon our canals as opportunities for leisure, but this was not why they were built, because in their heyday in the early 1800s the canal was more important than road transport and the railways had not yet come into being. The 'cuts' as they were called were very important during the war and once again there was a labour shortage as more and more barges were required. Women proved to be very quick, firstly to operate a single fuelled barge and then to manoeuvre a number of mini barges, locally called Tom Puddings, which were towed behind. The origin of the name 'pudding' comes from the shape of these units when loaded and piled high with coal.

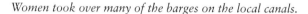

Women took over many of the barges on the local canals.

A barge pulling its train of Tom Puddings along the Leeds to Liverpool canal.

In the north-west of England these barges operated throughout the war on the Leeds and Liverpool and the Bridgewater canals, both of which had coal mines whose 'black gold' could be loaded directly by chutes into barges. Because diesel was at a premium, many barges were converted to run on coal and old steam-powered vessels were reconditioned and brought back into service. Horses were also brought back into service to tow the barges.

Modern writers have made the point that canal transport was too slow and could not operate in cold weather because of ice. Neither of these criticisms is justified. If bulk cargo is being carried, then the system is only as slow as the first load and in any case a barge and its puddings can deliver a huge tonnage. Secondly, in snow, canals do not get blocked

81

because the snow melts as it falls into the water. With regard to ice, the original builders of the canals had anticipated the problem. They devised specially constructed vessels called 'ice breakers', staffed by skilled men, and in the war by strong women. These teams operated in much the same way that road gritting teams operate today. They anticipated bad spells of weather and were on duty day and night whilst the cold weather lasted. The breakers were crewed by men with long-handled axes and sometimes bags of salt. On the Leeds to Liverpool canal the arches of the bridges had always been painted white to enable the bargees to navigate at night.

Marlene Jaques, then living in Burnley, recalls that the canal was used for leisure at least once during the war. The Sunday school held its annual 'bun fight' in a farmer's field that bordered the Leeds to Liverpool canal at the bottom of Barden Lane. A barge was cleaned up, decorated and used to give the children a trip for a short distance along the canal.

During the war the railway goods yards and the canal wharfs were almost choked with traffic and there was a logistical problem of moving goods to the point at which they were needed. With fuel shortages there could be only one solution. This was to use the horse, and the work of the carter was vital. Just as on the farms, the horse in the town was vital to the war effort.

Eric Wilson was a carter operating out of Liverpool docks, and shortly before he died in 1980 he recalled: "'Osses! I love 'em. I had two in the war. One I called Winston 'cos it used to whinny a lot and the other was a bad tempered bugger and I called him Adolf. Winston worked the day shift and Adolf worked at night. In May 1941 I was around the docks moving timber in the cart when the bombs struck. We were all shivering with fright as the fires started but Adolf never flinched. He then moved towards a burning building and I thought he had gone mad. He had a drink of water from a burst pipe and then set off towards home and his stable. I looked at my watch by the light of the fires and it was five minutes after his knocking off time. After that I called him Dolf – an 'oss that brave should not be saddled with a name like Adolf bloody Hitler.'

There are similar stories of horses doing their job in the face of noise, fire and danger, but it was the work that they did throughout Britain keeping deliveries flowing that should be celebrated. Coal, milk, foodstuffs, and even some munitions, were all delivered by horse and cart. The trite statement that horses did the donkeywork should never be underestimated. They had to be watered and fed and what goes in must come out. In the days of Dig for Victory their droppings also provided an invaluable supply of essential fertiliser!

So far I have described the transport systems operating during the war, but in those days by far the majority of people made their own way to work. Most people living in Lancashire towns at this time remember the early morning sound of clogs clattering on the cobbled streets and the swish of bicycle tyres as people went to and from work. Add to that the cheerful voices as workers greeted each other or exchanged news. The banter of mill lasses relating the news of a new boyfriend, an engagement, wedding or a birth was a typical sound when walking to work. The location of the cotton mills had not changed, even though many workers were now employed in the production of weapons or munitions.

Britain was coping well at this time but help was badly needed. This eventually came as the Americans entered the war. Many came in via Liverpool and this put extra strain on the transport system. But thank God that the Yanks did come – their contribution to the Lancashire war effort is the subject of the next chapter.

Chapter 4

The Atlantic Bridge

The 1930s had been bleak times for those employed in the building trades; bricklayers, joiners, plumbers and labourers could not find work during the depression. The onset of war provided not only conscripts for the armed services but also a reservoir of eager workers needed to build such things as airfields, camps for the armed forces and air raid shelters.

In the context of the North-West there was a real bonus in 1941 when the Americans joined the war. On this side of the 'Atlantic Bridge' was Liverpool. Through Liverpool came men and machines in staggering quantities. In particular there were aircraft, some crated up, some already assembled. The Americans needed spaces to assemble the planes, test them, repair them and fly them between Lancashire and the operational airfields on the eastern coast of England – facing Germany and occupied Europe. The result was two huge air bases, built at Warton near Blackpool and at Burtonwood near Warrington.

In these two areas of open countryside were constructed

what amounted to towns occupied by at least 10,000 men. Both had to be built from scratch! Furthermore they had to be up and running before the arrival of the troops who needed housing, feeding and entertaining, and as they were assembling and repairing several types of aircraft they also needed huge working areas. In addition they had to have airfields from which to fly the machines to the fighting units.

In 1999 I visited Frank Thomas, the architect of Warton airbase. Frank now lives in retirement in the Farnborough area but he was born in Blackpool and made his name as an architect of commercial aerodromes prior to the war. He told me how it all came about: 'I was involved in the selection of Warton, which the Americans wanted because it was further away from the dangers of bombing from German aircraft operating from France and the Low Countries. The most important factor, however, was the close proximity to Liverpool Docks. This was way back in 1940 and at that

The Yanks at work – Warton, 1943.

time America was not in the war but a lot of high ranking people knew that they would become involved sooner rather than later, and they planned accordingly. Thank goodness!

'As my family were from Blackpool I had a preference for Warton anyway, but Burtonwood was also ideal. All that was at Warton at that time was an open stretch of marshland. I was told to build an air maintenance base for 12,000 people and as this would be a small town it was obvious that a lot of local labour, both skilled and unskilled, would have to be brought in. Many plumbers, carpenters and bricklayers had to be placed in the reserved occupation category in order for this construction to be completed on time. Typical of how the ministries worked meant that there was a delay before I could really get cracking and so it was late in 1941 before work commenced. At that time there was only one dilapidated wooden hut, about 100 ft long, on the site with one old man living in it on his own.

'From late 1941 Lord Beaverbrook took charge and he was determined that I should build well and build fast. Beaverbrook was a bundle of energy and although born in Canada he was a great British patriot. Not only was he the Minister for Aircraft Production but he had also an extra incentive. His son, who later became Sir Max Aitken, was a decorated Spitfire pilot at the time of the Battle of Britain. Anybody who did not listen to Beaverbrook was sacked and I had no restraints placed on me either from a financial or a construction standpoint. Beaverbrook had been told by the Americans that they wanted to be in occupation at Warton by 1942. My instructions from him were simple: "Move fast or be sacked." This certainly kept my mind focused and I was equally firm with the civilian contractors.

'It helped that Beaverbrook told me face to face that money was no object. By November 1941 almost all the land required had been purchased. At this time I found out just how determined Beaverbrook could be. I was frequently visited by his underlings when we discussed progress and I wrote reports and requests. Then Beaverbrook came himself and he asked questions, barked orders, and made decisions on the spot. A local farmer had asked for more compensation money and the accountants were preparing to negotiate a deal, which was holding up progress. Beaverbrook said, "If he's still being difficult shoot him. If it's the accountant holding you up, shoot the bloody accountant." You knew where you were with Beaverbrook and because of his backing I was able to make very quick progress. I had no option but to move fast or I would have been out of a job!

'It may surprise people to know that my brief was not just to build quickly but I had to keep to the correct specifications as laid down by what was known as British Standards, which were actually the best in the world. I not only had to concentrate on the working hangars but also on living accommodation and to keep young men happy in sickness and in health. So I designed a theatre, cinema, areas of entertainment and a fully equipped hospital. Many of these buildings are still in use today and part of the BAe Systems operation which now constructs the Typhoon. So, long before the first Americans arrived, the local people already had an affection for the camp, with men and women employed there in large numbers.

'This friendly feeling continued after the Americans came and I remember clearly an incident in 1943. It was planned to give a Christmas party for nearly a thousand local children on the base but transport was a problem. I went to see the civilian contractors, who were still working on site. The firm was McAlpines and the workers agreed to close down at noon so that their transport could be used for the children in the afternoon. McAlpines decided to pay the men's lost wages out of their own pockets. The men agreed to this and then put the money into a kitty to buy presents for the children. Anybody who thinks that there was conflict between the Americans and the locals should take notice of events such as this.'

Some sympathy should be spared for the Americans who came over the Atlantic in their thousands. The USA is so large that it is not surprising that its people were and still are to some extent, insular. Young men in their teens and early twenties joined up or were conscripted, and were crammed into ships which crossed the often stormy Atlantic. No sooner had they recovered from seasickness than they were loaded into lorries or buses and then into the crowded billets of Warton. Nearby was the seaside resort of Blackpool but here was a foreign country and would the natives be friendly?

Sergeant Ralph Scott, on a visit to Warton in the year 2000 when I spoke to him, recalled: 'It was explained to us that the British were a bunch of stuffed shirts with no sense of

Sergeant Ralph Scott in 1943, at work at Warton. Like many Yanks, Ralph has fond memories of Lancashire folk.

humour and who would not talk to you until you had been properly introduced. Once we got to Blackpool we found out that this was nonsense but we did have problems. One of the first things we had to do was to learn how to count the money. It's not so bad now you are on a decimal system but 60 years ago you had pounds, shillings and pence. This was explained to us but most of us soon forgot the lessons given by our officers. Imagine the problems your modern kids would have if they had to go back to this system. A shilling was worth twelve pennies and there were 20 shillings in a pound. We were not smart enough to convert this back into dollars.

'I remember getting onto a double-decker bus which took us from the airbase door to our first visit to Blackpool. The conductor came to us with a smile but spoke in a broad Lancashire accent that we only gradually got used to. He said what sounded like "Uh up hu up". I looked at my mate who shrugged and said, "I think he wants money." I got some coins and said, "How much?" The conductor said, "Uh hoo oash a hoo", and looked at my coins and selected some of the big brown ones, which we later knew were pennies. In the change we got smaller brown ones, which were halfpennies. You haven't lived until you've been an American just arrived in England who can't understand the accent, can't count the money and does not know what somebody wants him to do. When we got to Blackpool we had to use some more of the big brown things to buy beer, which was not ice cool like Budweiser but warm and with a high froth on top. Life was certainly different.'

The Americans soon learned to integrate and considering that 10,000 young men arrived over a matter of weeks there was very little trouble. Blackpool with its long tradition of the Wakes Holiday Weeks was used to a sudden influx of visitors, but to have a new town suddenly appear on its doorstep and likely to be there for years was something altogether different. The young men needed entertaining and

Regular exhibitions were held in town halls, like this one in Blackpool in 1944. Funds were raised for all aspects of the War Effort and involved civilians and the armed forces.

Blackpool did not disappoint them, although as per Frank Thomas's design brief, the base had its own impressive entertainment programme.

Ralph Scott takes up the story: 'We had the American Red Cross on site at Warton but our method of operation was different to that in Britain. The British Red Cross had an aspect of nursing associated with it but our girls were more intent on setting up what we called Arrow Clubs. Our Red Cross girls visited British girls and chaperoned them as they visited our bases and enjoyed dancing with our troops. The idea of the Arrow Clubs was to make them feel safe. Apart from the men, the girls were attracted by big names such as Glenn Miller and his band, plus Bob Hope, Bing Crosby and Joe Louis the boxer, although he was more of an attraction for the men.'

The relationship between the Americans and the locals was surprisingly good with just the odd skirmish, usually caused by too much beer or perhaps not enough when the Yanks drank a local pub dry much to the annoyance of the locals.

Even one of the greatest civilian tragedies in the whole of the war served to bring the Americans and the local people closer together, in a bond between the two that continues to this day. On 23rd August 1944 an American Liberator B-24 bomber was hit by a violent and unexpected storm and the aircraft crashed into the Trinity Church School at Freckleton. The damage and the death toll was horrendous and included all the crew plus 38 infant schoolchildren, which amounted to the loss of a whole generation. Margaret Hall, who was a pupil at the school at the time, recalls: 'Strangely enough it brought the whole community – Americans and Brits – together. There was no animosity and at the funeral everybody hugged each other without thinking about where they were from. Obviously we all felt for the children and their parents but there were also thoughts for the crew. Also killed were some American and RAF lads who were sheltering from the storm in a little cafe near the school.'

August 1944 brought a treat for Americans and a few British civilians as Glenn Miller and his orchestra played to rapturous audiences at Warton.

Apart from the dead there were also lots of injured children whose suffering touched the hearts of all, including many influential Americans. When Bing Crosby visited Warton he was told about the accident and as Sergeant Ralph Scott recalls: 'Bing went to the hospital and saw a little girl called Ruby Whittle. She was five years old and she was in bandages from head to foot with just a little bit of her mouth showing and the tips of her fingers. Bing went to her bedside and asked her if he could sing to her. She nodded but when he started to sing he just choked up. I think it was the only time in that man's career that he could not sing a note. He got up but when he got to the door he turned around and sang *White Christmas* and *Don't Fence Me In*. Two little lads called George and David who were not so badly injured

93

The aftermath of the Freckleton disaster.

Americans at the Sad Sack Café at Freckleton in 1942. The café was destroyed in the aircraft crash two years later.

did their best to join in.'

The Americans designed and built a Memorial Garden, which has been beautifully maintained to this day. American veteran troops still pay annual visits and are entertained by Freckleton folk, but obviously as time passes fewer and fewer are left to remember the time they spent at Warton.

Warton was one of the largest American bases in Britain and rivalled only by Burtonwood near Warrington. Warton was known as BAD 2 and Burtonwood as BAD 1 (Base Air Depots).

Burtonwood was capable of assembling and servicing 15,000 aircraft and flying them off to the battle stations. Here were a host of workers servicing the United States 8th, 9th, 12th and 15th Air Forces. At its peak, 18,500 service men and women worked on the base, which covered not only the UK but later also Europe, the Middle East and the Mediterranean. Originally built for the RAF, Burtonwood first worked on Spitfires, which were so vital during the Battle of Britain. At the same time Burtonwood Repair Depot, which was an entirely civilian operation, was using the airfield. Many workers commuted from Manchester to Burtonwood via special fleets of buses.

In 1942 the Americans, eager to get into the war, took over the base and the United States Army Air Force was in full control from 1943 until 1946. As at Warton, Burtonwood was virtually a town with all essential services purpose-built by civilian contractors.

With such a large number of young energetic servicemen resident, Burtonwood looked like a recipe for trouble and the surprise is that there was so little disruption. The silly phrase that the Yanks were 'over paid, over sexed and over here' was a gross insult to the people who came to Britain

The funeral of the schoolchildren killed at Freckleton, their tiny coffins carried by American servicemen.

to help us. It is to the credit of the north-western civilians and to the Americans that things worked out so well.

In 1946 when the Americans left for home, it was the last wartime base to be closed. This closure, however, was short lived, as the Berlin airlift of 1948 brought the Americans rushing back into potential action, this time against the Russians.

The base was not finally decommissioned until 1965 and there was a further period of inactivity but then the Americans once more took control and used Burtonwood as a base for supplying equipment into Europe. Later, Burtonwood had a role during the First Iraq War and then in supplying hardware to the Balkans.

In 1987 the Burtonwood Association was formed with the object of celebrating the men and women who worked at the base until its final closure in 1993. The number of American

Bing Crosby at Warton in 1944.

Even with the war in full swing, the Burtonwood scene of 1944 was still surprisingly rural. (BAD 1 and Colonel W.W. Ott)

service personnel and British civilians associated with the base is fast diminishing but the importance of Burtonwood should never be forgotten.

Both Warton and Burtonwood, which became the largest site of its type in Europe, demanded lots of space. The reason for this was to allow fully kitted out aircraft awaiting delivery to battle zones to be spread out in order to minimise the effects of any attack on the airfield. Some of the big bombers were flown directly from America to the fitting out areas but the fighters, which had less range, were brought in crates and then delivered from Liverpool Docks on trailers to Burtonwood, Warton and some to Speke, which is now Liverpool Airport.

From 1940 onwards, young aeroplane spotters were kept in a constant state of excitement, as John Kirkman, who was only ten at the time, recalled: 'I could draw quite well and I was kept busy with my pencil and notebook. I saw for the first time aircraft such as American-built Boston Lysanders, Buffalos, Magisters and Hampdens. On one memorable day when I played truant and went on my bike to the area close to Burtonwood I saw first a Spitfire and then an American Flying Fortress. My future brother-in-law was a keen aeroplane spotter and became a member of the Royal Observer Corps.'

The well-known aviation historian Harry Holmes was inspired by his sightings around Warton: 'In common with most wartime schoolboys I had an interest in aeroplanes and built the multitude of models issued by the now almost forgotten names of Skyleada, Airdya, Skyrover and other kit manufacturers. Up to 1943 I was content to do this but then I felt the desire to see real aircraft. My school holidays were spent in and around Blackpool. By the middle of 1943 I began to notice that, among the men in RAF uniforms, there appeared Americans. I then began to notice wonderful new aircraft. As part of my education my grandmother encouraged me to keep a diary.'

Harry's records show his improving skill in aircraft recognition and led to a career in the RAF and BAe Systems until his retirement.

Like Harry, I also had a collection of aircraft recognition books but from 1943 onwards the sightings of German aircraft were few and far between. Why neither Warton nor Burtonwood was not successfully attacked by the Luftwaffe is difficult to understand because they had all the relevant photographs at their disposal. A Junkers Ju 88 did attempt to attack Burtonwood with incendiaries on 6th September 1940 but little damage was inflicted. Civilians from Warrington heard bombers on their way to bomb Manchester or Liverpool, but Burtonwood was not attacked and neither was Warton, which was also conveniently close to Liverpool. Once again, the Luftwaffe had good maps of the areas.

American aircraft on the way from Liverpool Docks to Burtonwood. Note the Liverpool Overhead Railway in the background. (By courtesy of Flight Magazine)

Aircraft recognition books were familiar to many keen spotters during the 1940s!

Not all the Americans were military personnel. There were also some known as 'feather merchants', who provided civilian services. Local folk were surprised and amused to see Americans in cowboy boots and ten-gallon hats drinking in local pubs and trying to get to grips with eating fish and chips and even cups of tea! They worked hard on aircraft engine production and servicing.

American Red Cross Clubs provided entertainment to remind the workers of life at home and the same organisation took over buildings in Warrington, Manchester and Liverpool in order to keep the troops off the streets. On the whole the local people were tolerant but they were not pleased when one of their favourite pubs – the Limerick – was demolished, as a runway was lengthened to cope with the arrival of larger American aircraft.

Burtonwood is now confined to history, as the land is now earmarked for 'development', whatever that means. It represents, however, a proud chapter in American military and British civilian history.

As we have seen, the Americans and British learned to live together without too much trouble. Did the Americans have any internal disagreements of their own? Unfortunately they did, because 60 years ago racial segregation was normal practice in the American services. Black Americans were faced with more problems than their white counterparts and sadly the two were kept in separate camps.

There was a particularly ugly incident in 1943 at the Hob Inn, which is still a thatched building in Bamber Bridge on the outskirts of Preston. A group of black GIs were not aware that the pub's closing time was 10 pm. The barmaid refused to serve the troops after this time and a disagreement broke out. A couple of heavy-handed white American Military Police were soon on the scene and the resultant scuffle became a serious racial confrontation. The MPs then produced guns and at their camp in Mounsey Road up to a hundred black troops broke into the armoury and a gun battle went on into the night. A white officer was seriously injured and a black soldier was killed. The civilian population of the area was obviously confused and frightened, some even thinking that the Germans had invaded. The following day the black soldiers surrendered and later the ringleaders were court-martialled and some received jail sentences of up to 15 years.

Considering that there was an endemic racial discrimination policy in the USA at this time, the wonder is that these incidents were so few and far between. More than 60 years later this relatively minor event is still talked about locally. Mrs Muriel Sparks recalled: 'I remember my father coming home from the Hob saying that there was trouble brewing because some Americans (he did not say whether they were black or white) troops did not understand our licensing hours and wanted to drink after hours. He said that our police would sort it out, but of course the Americans brought in their own police and that sparked even worse trouble.'

On the whole, peace and harmony prevailed and the Yanks probably changed the lives of British people forever. They brought nylons for one thing, made of a new material named by combining New York (NY) and London (LON). The troops were generous to the British girls and they also brought jive into the dance halls. In America the word 'jive' meant something second rate, so there they called this energetic dance the jitterbug. The British version was initially not so skilful and was therefore called the jive.

Entertainment was the key to good relations and a sort of stress buster. This is the subject of the next chapter.

Chapter 5

Fighting for Food

British farming in the late 1930s was to say the least in something of a desperate state. Farmers had either not been able to afford to update agricultural machinery or were not inclined to move away from practices which had hardly changed for centuries. Tom Case, who farmed near Preston, told me: 'Farms were small and mixed. I had sheep, cows, pigs, hens and areas of grassland. We could not afford a tractor and we sold our own meat, eggs and potatoes and my dad and me had a milk round. On the way home from selling the milk by horse and cart we cleaned windows and mended fences. After this was done we mucked out and at certain times of the year we ploughed.'

Mike Jackson, whose father had a farm in the Fylde area, recalled: 'My wife could buy foreign produced grain cheaper than I could grow it mesel.' Once we were at war, and could no longer rely on foreign imports, food production became vitally important and the old ways of farming had to change, voluntarily or by compulsion from the government.

Suddenly, farm workers were seen as the skilled

professionals they were. Farmers and their labourers had not been respected and were often regarded as unintelligent and possessed of few if any skills. There were, however, plenty of bright folk working in agriculture, as indeed they had to be in order to survive in a very competitive and declining market. Mike continued: 'I had an uncle who farmed in Sussex and his letters when the war started showed us that an invasion was not only possible but also probable. We thought we were safe here in Lancashire but we were soon made aware that an invasion force of Germans might well come via southern Ireland. I was twelve at the time and my dad wanted to join the army, as he had served in the first war. He was told in no uncertain terms that the best way he could help to win the war was to fight food shortages.

A familiar scene in the Lake District and Lancashire during the war years, with a combination of steam traction and horses ensuring that the harvest of hay was brought in, although obviously very labour intensive. This photograph shows men at work – they soon had to be assisted by the ladies!

He could join the Home Guard in his spare time but his ploughing skills were of much more use.

'In the early days of 1940 men in suits with posh accents arrived in big cars and carried notebooks. They measured and wrote down the number of acres each farm had. I know now these were called War Agricultural Committees but we thought they were interfering buggers who knew nowt about farming. We were wrong because most of us were brown, weather beaten and used to the wide open air. We did, however, have closed minds to improvements. So perhaps we were far too green to be useful!'

Those men with notebooks had a very important job to do. They collectively produced a 1940s version of the Domesday Book of farming. They knew the size of every farm and could estimate how much of a particular crop could be produced. Each farmer was told what to produce and in what quantity.

Farmers were soon being paid better and more reliably than ever before in their lives but there was pressure on them to hit production targets. John Parker, who farmed in the Fylde, told me: 'They did pay well and quick but there was pressure on us. Lazy farmers and those who were not bright enough were evicted even from their own land. It is not well recorded but I know of a couple who lost their farms because they did not realise that idle farmers could lose us the war. I worked with my dad, grandad and four brothers. We always talked over our dinner and we really did think that we were fighting a war. We would no more cheat on the officials than we would accept running away from an enemy.'

It has been officially recorded that throughout Britain more than 15,000 farms were 'requisitioned' from farmers who regularly and seriously failed to meet targets. Between 1939 and 1940 two million extra acres were added to land under the plough; this was achieved despite coping with one of the coldest winters on record. The year 1941 was not quite so bad and the spring ploughing and planting offensive

Like lots of farmers, Tom Barr of Fleetwood looked out all his old machinery and set about its restoration. Tom is seen here in 1942.

Ted Bateson, who now lives in Alston in Cumbria, with his beloved hardworking tractor in 1942.

throughout Britain was more effective as management techniques improved.

Jonty Withers worked as a labourer throughout the war from his farm near Morecambe, and he told me: 'It's funny, I just wanted to get involved in farming and I kept notes of how things changed on the land. What would have happened to British agriculture if it had not been for the war I shudder to think! Changes which would have taken half a century took less than a year. Farmers became skilled engineers, horse fairs were replaced by machinery shows, which are still part of the Lancashire country scene today.'

My own memories involve seeing the arrival of huge new machinery and shiny tractors and watching as these monsters rooted out scrub and even substantial trees to make room for more land on which to grow crops. In 1939 there were fewer than 50,000 tractors in Britain but this figure had increased to more than 200,000 by 1945. Most farmers could not have afforded this financial outlay but they were funded by a desperate government, with American assistance.

Fordson tractors were treated like favourite horses and some were even given pet names. Henry Ford, the son of a farmer, had developed his Fordson tractor after the First World War. They modernised the farming industry and British farmers came to love them. The engine was simple and almost trouble-free. James Parr, who now runs a museum at his farm near Fleetwood, showed me one of his old tractors. This is the second oldest Fordson tractor still existing in the world. Built in 1919, it did sterling service during the war.

Mike Jackson pointed out: 'Growing for Victory became an obsession with us all. We knew that the tractor was the

Even in agriculture it was a case of adapting what you had – in 1940 this Austin Heavy Saloon of 1926 was modified to become a tractor. James Parr of Fleetwood calls this a 'half and half'.

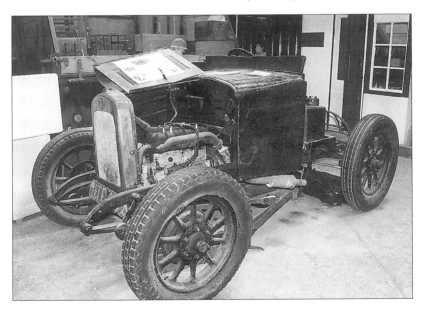

"workhorse" of the future but we did not abandon our heavy horses at this time. Indeed, we used both. The great thing about the tractors is we did not have to groom them before starting work in a morning or rub them down at the end of the day. The tractor's engine could be started at the push of a button, and it could operate all day from dawn to dusk. We even used our tractor on a shift basis. In 1943 we produced more food than had been grown in the first seven years of the 1930s. Only when we got tired did things change – instead of having too many idle and unskilled hands we all became desperate for more labour.'

Many men preferred to fight rather than farm. If there were not enough men to farm, then it became obvious that women had to take a hand. Enter the Land Army girls.

The Women's Land Army

Edith Ashborne, who is now 'well in her nineties', had a father in the East Lancashire Regiment killed in the First World War and had an auntie in London killed in a Zeppelin raid, and she was determined to do her bit this time round. 'I was living in Manchester, working in an office,' remembered Edith. 'When I saw an advert for the Land Army I was soon knocking on the door. I had enjoyed holidays in the countryside so I was not a typical Lancashire lass fresh from the city. I thought I knew all about country life. On my first day I was kicked by a horse and was off work for a week. I then tried to milk a reluctant cow, got nipped by a sheep dog and fell off the tractor. After that things got better. I got brown, made hay whether the sun shone or not and found a husband.'

Edith's story is fairly typical and no one should underestimate the contribution to the war effort made by the Land Army. George Myerscough, who worked as a farm labourer near Blackpool during the war, told me that some of the city girls adapted so quickly to tractor driving that 'I left them to it and I got on with ploughing with the horses that I

Posters like this brought many city girls into the Women's Land Army.

knew so well.' City girls were thought to be 'fast' and Cyril Makepeace, who worked on a farm at Garstang, mentioned that 'local lasses were founder members of the resistance movement whilst the new beauties from the towns were at times smashing collaborators!'

Despite common belief, the Women's Land Army was not first formed in 1939. Actually it had its origins in the First World War. In 1917 Roland Prothero, the Minister for Agriculture, had looked at the losses of merchant vessels caused by the concerted action of U-boats and urged the formation of the Women's Land Army to increase the volume of home-produced food. At that time the young men of Britain were being slaughtered in their thousands as trench warfare paid for every inch of land with blood. Women were brought in to cultivate acres of land for much needed food. These ladies were then Britain's 'forgotten army' and they did not get the credit their efforts deserved either during the First or the Second World War.

Gladys Beacon from Wigan observed: 'We did not know we were a forgotten army but looked at half a century on I suppose we were. In 1939 I was just turned 18 and set to be a humble cotton operative in Manchester if I could get a job in the hard times of the 1930s. Then adverts for the Land Army started to appear all over the city. I was one of the first to join up and by late June 1939 I was sent to a farm near Clitheroe.'

There was initially no shortage of volunteers but soon there were other demands for the services of young women in Lancashire. Aircraft parts and munitions needed nimble hands and the ability to work in noisy conditions. Audrey Hepworth, who was born in Burnley, told me: 'In the mills we all learned to speak what we called "mee-mo". It was a sort of lip reading, which cut out the need to speak above the machinery. It was not a sign language as such because you cannot use your hands at the same time as operating machinery.'

By 1944 the labour shortage was such that conscription was necessary and at the end of that year some 80,000 fit (in the old fashioned use of the word) lasses were working on the land. It was not just working girls who turned their hand to hoe, scythe, tractor and plough. The Land Army cut straight across the then quite rigid class barriers. Lady Wotnot's daughter got just as mucky as Elsie Blogg's lass from the slums of Salford. The barriers were eroded by the wearing of a uniform - each girl was issued with a pair of Wellington-type boots and a pair of stout shoes along

Land Army uniform of 1942, displayed on a model at the Millom Air Museum and looking neat and glamorous – not the experience of all land army lasses!

with two pairs of socks and a couple of pairs of breeches. Each had a hat, two short-sleeved shirts and a green pullover. Seen in black and white photographs today the uniform looks dull, but at the Millom Air Museum the kit has been cleaned, pressed and displayed on a model and looks neat and surprisingly colourful.

The girls themselves, however, did not feel glamorous. 'The

113

thing we all hated most was the winter waterproof. It was very thin and didn't even keep the rain out,' said Jackie Nield, a miner's lass from Wigan who worked on a farm on the Fylde. 'I remember being cold and homesick and although I could not write reet well in them days I sent a sort of wish list to my mum. She found some old woollen clothes which were green. She pulled this back and knit it thick and warm. All I had to do was to stitch on my badges.' Some girls complained about having to wear a tie and rough aertex shirt.

There was an enforced form of discipline in the WLA but this also served to protect the girls from any unscrupulous employer. Each county had an elected representative and an organising secretary and they could deal with disputes and complaints. There was even an official song:

> Back to the land, we must all lend a hand,
> To the farms and the fields we must go.
> There's a job to be done,
> Though we can't fire a gun,
> We can still do our bit with the hoe...
> Back to the land with its clay and its sand,
> Its granite and gravel and grit.
> You grow barley and wheat
> And potatoes to eat,
> To make sure that the nation keeps fit....
> We will tell you once more,
> You can help win the war,
> If you come with us – back to the land.

Jackie Nield remembered: 'We all knew the song but we added rude words to it so often that we could not remember the clean version. When visitors came, especially the press, we had to carry the words on a sheet. At one time there was a rumour that Lord Beaverbrook was coming to visit us so we all had to learn the words proper-like. We were all so bloody good that we sounded like a choir. Then he did not turn up.'

The Land Army girls were hard workers, especially in the warmer months when double summer time was in force and it was a dawn to dusk day during harvest time. There were, however, also opportunities to play hard. 'We went to the pictures a lot at night but we often had to walk as much as four miles unless somebody lent us bikes. This was no joke after lighting up time and I ended more than one journey in a muddy ditch,' recalled Edith Ashborne. 'We also got the chance to go to local village dances.'

Jackie Nield and her friends were luckier than most: 'We were not far away from the Yank camp at Warton and there were thousands of them there – it were like a town. They were short of lasses and always provided us with transport there and back. There were some hanky panky but neither us nor the Yanks were as loose in morals as is often said. Most on 'em were just lonely lads and some of us hadn't seen a good-looking lad for a couple of years. I once tried to

Miss M. Palmer kept her badges and her letter recording her service in the Women's Land Army, signed by the Queen.

stop one lad reaching under my coat only to find when I got home there was a parcel – it was a case of grub, not grope! We all shared cake and a rib of beef on the next day.'

Lillian Parker, born in Rochdale, remembers her Land Army days high in the hills over the Irwell Valley. 'I had led a somewhat sheltered life with overseas holidays and the use of one of several family cars. My elder sister and I shared a maid and I can never remember running my own bath. On my first day as a Land Army recruit I met a rough Lancashire lass from Oldham named Ann Harding. Ann had always gone to the municipal baths once a week or else used the tin bath in front of the fire. Within a couple of days we were as thick as thieves and along with a couple of other girls (one eventually became a vet) there was nothing we liked better than to share a hot tub at the end of a cold winter's day. We also ate quite well with stews and lots of vegetables, which we planted and later gathered ourselves. On one memorable occasion when it was my birthday a delicacy known as scrag end of lamb appeared. I'd not been used to this but what a feast it was, all soaked up with home-baked bread. At the end of the war Ann and her husband (he was Polish and she met him in the war) came to work for me when I inherited my house because my brothers were all killed in the war. Nicholas drove the car and kept the garden whilst Ann was the cook. We were really still just friends and she was wonderful at cooking broth and scrag end. This is what the Land Army did – it broke down class barriers which should not have been there in the first place!'

It is easy to romanticise the past and, after half a century, the backbreaking work and the pressure of fighting for food and victory fades a little. It was a delight, however, to record the thoughts of these lasses with their 'down to earth' (literally) commonsense.

'We had a job to do but when you are young you do not live in the past or think of the future,' said Sylvia Worsley. 'I came from Ashton-under-Lyne originally and I was a townie

Haymaking at Heysham in the 1940s.

when I joined the Land Army. These days we have huge farms but they are all what they call "monocultures". I went to work on an old-fashioned mixed farm. If you go to a toyshop and buy a children's farm you will have a farmhouse building and outhouses consisting of dairy, milking parlour, stables, a pigsty and lots of hens grubbing about – that's what farms were like then. Birds, mice and even rats were everywhere and the local cats and assorted dogs kept nature in balance. In the surrounding fields sheep and cattle grazed whilst horses rested from their labours. The beloved tractor was the most prized possession. I soon became an "animal" person but I was allowed to drive an old Leyland truck which had been made less than three miles away from the farm. I had to do a round collecting waste food (which there was not much of) and mixing this as food for the pigs. Potato peelings and caterpillar and slug-chewed cabbage leaves were all welcome. I guess they even got lots of slugs mixed in with the swill. I remember spending a half-day in the woods with a fella. Guess what? In the autumn of 1942 we collected a huge number of acorns, which we fed to the pigs. They loved 'em. That year there was a glut of mushrooms. There were so many that we even shared these with the pigs. It really was a case of waste nowt in those days.'

Gladys Cottom, who was born in Wigan but now lives in Australia, also has fond memories of her life as a Land Army lass: 'I joined in 1941 and was sent off to an agricultural college near Nantwich in Cheshire. I enjoyed the month-long training course, during which I learned to milk a cow. We first practised on a leather and canvas udder hung from a wooden frame, which was guaranteed not to kick or lash its tail. I was lucky in that I could already drive a car and was taught to operate an ever-reliable Ferguson tractor, which I operated until the end of the war. I was also driven into the arms of an Aussie who had joined RAF Bomber Command in 1940 and to whom I have been married for more than 50 years. He fought from the air and I fought literally from ground level.'

Dig for Victory

The huge amounts of land brought into food production was enterprise on a large scale. On a more parochial scale, every able-bodied person was encouraged to Dig for Victory.

Dig! Dig! Dig! and your muscles will grow big,
Keep on pushing the spade.
Don't mind the worms,
Just ignore their squirms,
And when your back aches laugh with glee.
And keep on diggin',
Till we give our foes a wiggin'.
Dig! Dig! Dig! to Victory.

George Myerscough told me: 'When I were a lad in Wigan I had a broad local accent. To us in school our town name

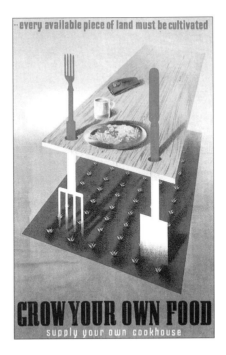

'Dig! Dig! Dig to Victory'!

was "Wiggin" and we thought that the *Dig for Victory* song was written just for us!'

I suppose we now take these slogans for granted but it is hard to overestimate the value of humorous songs and poems and also the colourful posters which appeared almost immediately after war was declared. In my Lake District school at Askam near Barrow-in-Furness, for example, we had our very own garden. Our teacher was Gordon Ramsey, who could bowl a cricket ball at high speed and also had an artistic talent, and was not slow to operate a spade. He drew a map of part of our playing field and without interfering with the football space marked out a garden. Each youngster was allocated into teams of four and was given planting instructions. We had to find out as much as we could about the crop we were to cultivate. I was eight when I realised that cabbage, Brussels sprouts and cauliflower were parts of the same plant. The sprouts were the buds, cabbage the leaves and the 'cauli' was literally the flower! Over the years the three vegetable types were developed. I don't think I am stretching the truth too far to say that this was a centuries-old example of genetic engineering!

We also collected posters and were encouraged to draw our own version to take home to proud parents. Many children learned to read and write thanks to Potato Pete:

> Here's the man who ploughs the fields,
> Here's the girl who lifts up the yield,
> Here's the man who deals with the clamp,
> So that millions of jaws can chew and champ.
> That's the story and here's the star,
> Potato Pete!
> Eat up, eat up.
> Ta Ta! Ta Ta!

This was set to music and sung with great success by Betty Driver, the Lancashire comedienne. She later became famous as *Coronation Street*'s Betty Turpin. Nursery rhymes were soon adapted.

> Jack Spratt could eat no fat,
> His wife could eat no lean,
> So they both ate potatoes
> And scraped their platters clean!

Doctor Carrot also did a 'reet grand job'. The doctor told us how healthy carrots were. They can be grown so easily that they were used as a substitute for almost anything, including sugar because of their natural sweetness. Carrots were added to cakes and carrot jam proved to be very popular. The wife of a friend of mine who is as thin as a lath but thinks she is fat goes on regular visits to a health farm. She is charged a lot of money for her daily dose of carrot juice. This set me thinking of drinking something similar, produced from vegetables from our school garden. It was called 'carrotade' and was made by squeezing the juice from carrots and swede. What was left of the vegetables was boiled and eaten. There is, it seems, nowt new under the sun!

The Dig for Victory campaign was not just an exercise to boost the morale of the people but it was essential to keep us all fed and did actually work. Initiated in 1939, progress on the campaign was dramatically quick and accelerated to such an extent that by 1943 it was estimated that over one million tons of vegetables were being produced in gardens and allotments.

As already mentioned, most schools had their own plots, and huge numbers of families with gardens were hard at it. Those with back yards either dug up the hardcore or planted edible crops in pots or boxes. Even in the heart of cities such as Liverpool and Manchester, vegetables were grown and in many cases bombsites were taken over. There was one such 'grow your own' area in Manchester city centre and another alongside a huge railway marshalling yard at Rosegrove, near Burnley. Keith Emmett, who was a schoolboy in Burnley in the 1940s, remembers seeing cabbages being grown close to rail trucks loaded with tanks and armaments on their way from Leeds to Liverpool Docks.

Lancashire must have been one of the counties best equipped to 'Dig for Victory'. The miners, cotton operatives and workers in heavy industry were used to spending their days in noisy, dirty and unhealthy conditions. For more than a century they had been urged to get into the fresh air as often as they could and most working men had their own allotment. Some kept their own hens and many, especially miners, kept ferrets, which were skilled at catching rabbits to supplement the meat ration. These men had long taken pride in their allotments, hen pens and pigeon lofts, which were passed on from father to son.

Digging for victory in the centre of Piccadilly in Manchester. Note the air raid shelter in the background.

Wilf Jaques and his daughter Marlene on their allotment in the early 1940s.

Cotton workers like Wilf Jaques built their own cooking stoves, which they fuelled with garden rubbish, thus saving the coal or coke used at home. Wilf's daughter, Marlene, recalls: 'I was born in 1938 and I can never remember Dad without his allotment. During the war there was a real community spirit "down at the pen". We sheltered from the rain in the greenhouse and were protected from the wind by fences, which were also used to support climbing stems of beans and Dad even grew sweet peas. He was quite well known for these flowers, which gave such a show that travellers on the nearby railway used to look out of the windows to admire them. I can still conjure up the sweet smell of these and I love the taste of broth made from fresh vegetables.'

Very young children were encouraged to grow vegetables in their own patch and were allowed to grow a few flowers in between rows. Betty Parton's father was a builder in St Helens and he grew crops in every inch of space. She remembers to this day the aroma of fresh peas and broad beans.

As a seven-year-old I learned to like carrots and cauliflower because I had grown them myself. Many northern gardeners entered competitions and were proud of prize-winning onions, marrows and especially leeks. The peacetime garden shows continued during the war and provided even more of a competitive spirit, especially in villages where rivalry had always been almost as fierce as warfare! Villagers soon got used to town-based 'spivs' raiding their allotments for produce to sell on the black market. Pups were taught to bark and bite whilst old men and youths patrolled their fruit and veg areas, often carrying sticks and paper bags full of pig manure, which they could throw with great accuracy! Strange vans were monitored, had their tyres deflated and the local policeman was added to the garden anti-invasion force.

There was very little difference between gardening and farming. Gerald Rawstron of Great Harwood, near Blackburn, recalls: 'June to August brought hay-making. Generally our local farms weren't mechanised and so there was plenty of work on offer. Children like us would join the farm labourers and we turned the hay so that it dried in the sun. We used rakes which were about 2 ft 6 ins wide with teeth made from wooden pegs. After all the grass had been cut, mostly by old timers who had a lifetime of experience in operating the scythe, there was the tidying up to do. The day after we began to rake the grass into stacks we had developed a rhythm. Periodically, but not often enough for us, the farmer would come out with a huge jar full of sarsaparilla. If we started early in the morning it would be before the hay was dry. Then came a supply of cheese sandwiches, a piece of cake and a big mug of tea and then it was back to work. We all learned to make the best of the weather and on good days we might not finish until 10 pm. I don't think we were paid very much but the food was good, with rationing regulations usually overlooked by the farmer, who made his own butter and cheese. Eggs appeared as if by magic!'

In the 1930s and the 1940s communities were more self-sufficient than we are today and this applied particularly to villages. The Harvest Festival was one occasion when the church took the lead and people gave their thanks for their food, and this came to have special meaning during the war. During late October and mid-November many villages held Harvest Suppers, which were sometimes called Harvest Homes. These I remember very well. My mother told me that this was traditionally the time to enjoy country food, such as a Lake District potato pie cooked with beef or mutton. But what happened between 1939 and 1945 and even beyond when rationing was more strictly applied? Most villages carried on and adapted. People saved up their rations and what became known as 'Jacob's Joins' were popular events when everyone brought what they could and the best cooks in the village worked wonders. My aunt Millie was a real miracle worker at these feasts. With the Dig for Victory campaign in full swing the suppers were a triumph for the ingenuity of local folk. Tins of corned beef were charmed from the shelves of local grocers, while chunks of beef, mutton or pork came from farm kitchens, usually with the full blessing of the local bobby.

If this was stretching the law just a little for the sake of

FIGHTING FOR FOOD

community spirit, there were also legally acceptable ways of enjoying food. Fruits such as apples and pears were made into pies sweetened using locally available honey, and rabbits were common and regarded as a pest, but very good in a pie! All these 'free' bounties were gratefully accepted.

My old school friend, the late John Walker at Askam-in-Furness, told me: 'I know that the vicar, the Reverend Chair, provided vegetables for the harvest supper from his own garden. The supper was held either in the school hall or the band hall. The local Silver Band provided music and local folk sang. Being a coastal village, flat fish, cockles and shrimps were an added bonus to our diet. It has to be remembered that there was no way at that time that food could be frozen and a barter system was soon in operation. I often exchanged fish that I caught one day for a rabbit which would be delivered in the near future.'

I too have memories of the way this barter system, which was perfectly legal, worked. I was eight years old in 1944 and had been taught how to swim, but also to be afraid of an incoming tide. Because of this, like most village children, I was given more independence than might be the case today. John Walker, and especially my Uncle Billy, taught me how to catch fish by a method called 'bank-lining'. On Askam's sandy beach at that time were solid wooden stakes pushed into the mud and sand, meant to prevent the landing of any invading force arriving by sea. These provided an anchor for a long line with fishhooks placed at intervals of about a foot. We could cope with about 70 hooks, each of which was baited with lugworm. Whilst we were digging for bait we gathered cockles which were eaten for supper. All this was done at low water.

We then went home for the period of high tide. As the sea ebbed we harvested the bank line. We never had fewer than ten fish, usually flat fish, which fed the family. I once caught 48 flat fish and two sea bass, which meant that there was a surplus to be got rid of. None of us had even heard of a fridge. Then the barter system came into smooth operation. Out came my bike and off I went on a tour of local farms. I came home from Harry Bird's farm with a piece of cheese, a slab of butter and two rashers of fatty bacon. There were also two eggs wrapped in a protective layer of hay. From the vicar I got a lovely pie made with russet apples sweetened with honey. One sea bass for Farmer Askew who lived near Dunnerholme between Askam and Kirkby produced two rabbits.

At low water we would seek out pools that formed in depressions in the sand. Here I learned to tread for flat fish. This meant paddling in bare feet and feeling the wriggling fish with my toes. Many years later whilst making a television film for Granada Television with the presenter Bob Smithies, I found that I still had the knack to catch 'flatties'!

I also went on my bicycle to watch the shrimpers at work in Morecambe Bay. They would often let us youngsters help to arrange the nets. Years later I spoke to Harold Benson whose family have caught shrimps in Morecambe Bay for more than 200 years. Harold told me: 'Nobody in Flookborough went

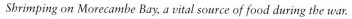

Shrimping on Morecambe Bay, a vital source of food during the war.

Harold Benson in the 1970s demonstrating the art of making a living from the sea during the war years.

129

short in the war. We lived off shrimps, fish and vegetables. We even had enough spare to sell to the local airfields where they trained pilots. We could often exchange a supply of sea food for a bottle of whisky or a few fags.'

In other villages of the north-west similar bartering took place. Enid Dawson, whose uncle lived near Windermere, told me: 'The old man was nearly 80 then and he had fished all his life. He caught trout and salmon in rivers (how legal this was I don't know) and he had an old rowing boat that he kept on the lake. He caught perch and pike and his wife had mouth-watering recipes for all types of fish. He had a damson orchard and a garden with lots of beehives in it. He grew every vegetable you could think of. When he had anything to barter he walked miles around local farms and returned with eggs, butter, cheese, bits of fatty bacon and on one wonderful occasion, a chicken. Although it was July 1943 we were all invited to join him for what turned out to be an out of season Christmas dinner. Old Victor lived to be over 90 and in 1949 he showed me a place on the banks of Windermere where they built Sunderland Flying Boats during the war. Next to this was a factory where they processed perch. This was mixed with tomato sauce, tinned and marketed under the brand name of Perchines.'

Whilst such activities were mainly focused around the rural areas, some townies were able to live off the land, and reservoir keepers had to be on the guard as a free fish supper was a welcome addition to the rations. These days the water companies often welcome anglers but this is a very recent concession. Anyone even walking close to a reservoir before the 1970s could expect a hostile reception from the water bailiff, who was often armed with a shotgun, especially during the war.

The work of farmers, the Land Army girls, the Dig for Victory campaign and the ingenuity of civilians meant that rationing did not bite as hard as was feared. Shortages of everything, however, were suffered as part of the war effort.

Chapter 6

Coping with the shortages

Being an island nation and a small one at that, there was no way that Britain could have fed itself even if the Dig For Victory campaign and the Land Army lasses had worked miracles. As war became inevitable, plans were made to instigate a rationing scheme that would be fair to all.

In 1937 the Ministry of Food was set up in preparation for the rationing of some goods immediately should war be declared. There were several departments within the ministry, each with responsibilities for different categories of food and other products.

Long before the war started local Food Offices had been designated. In order to obtain a product there were two essential requirements. These were coupons and money. The ration book is now part of any museum exhibit or publication relating to the 1940s. It looks simple – one ration book for each individual. People were ordered to register with the shops of their choice – butcher, grocer and perhaps dairy. They handed over their book to the proprietor who

clipped out the appropriate coupon. Minnie Jaques, who had a draper's shop on Abel Street, Burnley, during the war, remembers having to take the clothing coupons she had collected from customers and hand them in to the bank for checking. However, there was more than one kind of ration book.

A green ration book enabled pregnant women, nursing mothers and children under five to go to the front of the queue. They could have the first choice of bananas and oranges if these fruits became available. They could also have a daily pint of milk and a double supply of eggs.

Children between five and sixteen years of age had a blue ration book, which meant that they were allowed fruit as and when available, a full meat ration and half a pint of milk daily. The standard buff coloured ration book was issued to all other adults, who had to make do with basic rations.

Rationing did not start until January 1940, with bacon, sugar and butter. Meat restrictions followed in March and, in July, tea was rationed to 2 ounces per person per week. When the Ministry of Food issued Bulletin No 3, dated June 1940, they pointed out: 'We should all use less tea. If each of us gives up one teaspoonful in four we shall have shipping space for 50,000 tons of war material in a year. This is a war contribution which one and all should make.'

Margaret Coates of Rochdale recalls: 'My mother gave me the job of straining the tea leaves and drying them off on the kitchen range. The tea could then be reused. It was a fiddling job but there were no tea bags in those days.'

After tea came a strict rationing allocation relating to cooking fats, cheese, conserves and eggs (one per person per week). During the war only so-called 'solid cheese' could be made. This was because it could be more easily stored and cut without crumbling. The crumbly forms would have resulted in a lot of waste.

Fish was not rationed but was often scarce and attracted long queues. The Ministry of Food introduced a dairy replacement in the form of dried milk, which came in tins. Each family was allowed one tin per month, which was the equivalent of four pints.

Lord Woolton, the Minister of Food, declared that it was his job 'to see that everyone received

Shortages soon began to bite once war had been declared.

Spam and dried eggs were a wholesome feature of many wartime breakfasts.

the minimum amount of protein and vitamins to ensure good health under hard working conditions.'

It is an interesting exercise for anyone who wants to understand what rationing meant, to take a look at their weekly supermarket shopping and compare it to what could be obtained in January 1940. One week's supply of groceries, for instance, was limited to 4 ounces of ham or bacon, 12 ounces of sugar and 4 ounces of butter. Allowances, however, did fluctuate throughout the war depending upon available supplies.

Despite shortages of meat there were some cuts which people found not to their taste. Horsemeat was tolerated, but as Ann Fearnley of Rochdale told me: 'Nobbut just, but none of us would eat whale meat, which was far too black and oily. I once tried a tin of snoek, which was a fish from South Africa brought in just as the war was ending. It was supposed to taste like tinned sardines but none of us would eat it.'

Retrospective evidence suggests that poorer families actually benefited from rationing because prices were also strictly controlled. Some of the rich did resort to the illegal black market but the poor were at least sure of their ration at an affordable price.

Some people with spare cash stockpiled non-perishable goods before the war began, as Mrs Joyce Kershawe of Manchester told me: 'My parents were quite forward looking and prior to the onset of war they bought a full chest of tea and two one-hundredweight sacks of sugar. They also stocked up on tins of fruit, meat and fish. These were only used on special occasions such as Christmas and birthdays. There were two tins of meat they were determined not to

Millions of tons of South African snoek were imported at the end of the war. Most people did not like the taste and would not eat it.

Nothing was wasted – if people would not eat it, the pigs would!

use – a seven-pound tin of corned beef and a seven-pound tin of corned mutton. These were kept until the war ended. My mother put on a street party on VE Day and we had beef, mutton, tinned fruit cocktail, peaches, pineapple and pears, plus lots of jellies. We saved some for VJ Day and our neighbours were over the moon.'

The Kershawes were not alone in being prepared because they were following government advice. During the preparations for war huge volumes of paperwork were generated, including a Civil Defence Public Information Leaflet dated July 1939; its subheading was much more to the point – *Your Food in Wartime*. This laid down a series of important facts and guidelines relating to rations for those who remained at home and those who were evacuated because of safety or the government's dictates relating to employment, beginning: 'Our country is dependent to a very large extent on supplies of food brought from overseas. More than 20 million tons are brought into our ports from all parts of the world in the course of a year. Our defence plans must therefore provide for the protection of our trade routes ... During the last eighteen months the Government has purchased considerable reserves of foodstuffs which are additional to the commercial stocks normally carried.'

The leaflet then went on to suggest that householders should do some stockpiling, advice which those like the Kershawes quickly acted upon. It was recognised, though, that not everyone had the spare cash to stockpile. In each area food control was to be the responsibility of a local committee, which would start to operate on the day that war was declared. On these committees were well respected shop owners, and lists of shopkeepers were compiled from those given a licence to trade. In those days almost every street had its corner shop and so the control of food supplies was much easier than would be the case today. New shops would only be licensed if the committee felt it to be necessary. Obviously this did happen when workers were brought into industrial sites and billeted in specially constructed blocks or in hotels or private houses. This certainly was the case in the seaside resorts of Lancashire where large numbers of civil servants were evacuated away from the Blitz of the large cities.

The paperwork involved in this scale of organisation was enormous and it is no wonder that newspapers were reduced in size and that paper began to be recycled. Before rationing began, forms were sent through the post to each householder, who had to provide a list of all who were in residence. These forms, which amounted to a total population census, were sent to the Local Food Control Committee. This committee issued the relevant ration books and these also contained the name and address of the supplier. This avoided some shops having no stocks left whilst others had more than they needed.

There were plans in place to check up on those suppliers who gave short weight and sold their ill-gotten surplus to the black market. Some shoppers were asked at random to pass their purchases on to an official who would check the weight of the goods and then return them to the customer. This scheme was soon common knowledge among the shopkeepers and very few were prepared to take the risk.

Local folk knew who the crafty crooks were and after the war when rationing was over they 'voted with their feet', so to speak, and the guilty soon went out of business. Ron Garner of Rochdale remembers the fate of one unscrupulous shopkeeper: 'Most grocers dealing with rations were fair but there was the occasional crook. Whenever word got around that something special had arrived at his shop a queue would soon form. He would allow you to buy, say, a pound of tomatoes or an orange if available providing you would also buy other items not on ration and usually potatoes at the price he decided upon. Needless to say, when the war ended and more shops became available his business collapsed.'

The same happened to a grocer in Bury, as Betty Lewthwaite, who was a barmaid during the war, recalled:

'Our local grocer was known to give short weight but was crafty enough to avoid getting caught. He loved his whisky, which, when we had available supplies, he drank. He often slipped us some sugar or butter but we always gave him short measure for his drinks. I suppose we were breaking the law just like he was. We had another customer who was old and had been badly injured in 1916 during the First World War. We gave him a free whisky and also the goodies given to us by the crooked grocer and so we felt our conscience was clear.'

Very few grocers were crooks and some were very benevolent as Don Woodhouse of Blackburn remembered: 'One abiding memory is the length of time it took to shop; my mother shopped at the Co-op which was in West End, a five-minute walk away. It often took two hours waiting her turn in the queue and as I got older I was sent and I remember that it took an age. I knew all the assistants and they would occasionally slip something in the basket whilst muttering "something extra". What amazes me now is that I never saw anyone lose their temper whilst waiting.' Alan Hargreaves, who lived in Dalton-in-Furness in 1942, recalls waiting in a long queue to buy two oranges.

I knew Tom Murphy in the early 1980s when he was about to retire from Hull's grocer's shop on School Lane in Brinscall, near Chorley. He was still loved by his customers when he was in his nineties, and many remembered how fair he was during the war. The late Benita Moore wrote a poem about old Tom:

Even through the trials of war,
Hull's village shop was there,
To make sure people got their dues
And all were fair and square.

Arthur Crabtree, the grocer at Stacksteads, near Bacup, had 290 customers when he was given six tins of salmon.

Tom Murphy in his nineties, just before retirement from Hull's grocery shop at Brinscall.

He put all the names in a hat and six customers were happy, although one of them complained that she did not get an 'A' quality tin!

As surplus stocks began, literally, to be eaten into as the war went on, rationing became ever more stringent. This applied especially to luxury items such as chocolate and sweets. Looked at in retrospect, more than 60 years on, it might seem that children would have felt deprived. This was not the case and Gerald Rawstron of Great Harwood echoes my own feelings of the time: 'During the war I did not notice a lack of food. As children we had never known anything different. In fact for many people food was more plentiful in spite of the rationing.

'For those who were spared HM Forces, because of age, infirmity or essential work, life was pretty good.

Unemployment during the recession of the 1930s had given way to full employment, which was often well paid especially in the munitions factories. Wives of those in the forces were often in work and augmenting the meagre allowances given by the government to the dependants of men away at the war. Even people who stuck to their ration either because of their principles or because they did not have the contacts or something to exchange on the black market were comparatively well fed. It has been said that the wartime rations in the 1940s probably provided the healthiest diet we have known. Vegetables and bread were easily available but you had to queue. As children we were often given extra from our parents' ration. My Uncle Fred had a hen pen and so we probably had more than our fair share of eggs and the occasional chicken – usually at Christmas. Even much later, well into the 1950s, chicken was an expensive delicacy, only eaten at Christmas and the New Year.

'On one occasion at school we were asked to contribute to the cost of a crop of bananas. We did not know what a banana tasted like but we were shown pictures. Unfortunately, we never got to have one. We were told that they were needed for sick children and were asked to give up our share. I have since wondered if the ship was sunk and we were not told. It is more likely to have been a morale booster.

'As soon as sweets were rationed I had to look after my own coupons, which was good for me. Even though my Aunt Betsie had a sweet shop I was kept strictly to my ration. The only way to exceed rations was to find somebody with coupons but no money. One supplied the coupons, the other the money and the sweets were shared equally. I suppose this was a sort of children's black market but so far as I know this practice was quite legal. It was some years after the war ended before sweets were taken off ration. There was then an immediate "greed rush" and they had to be re-rationed for some considerable time.'

Adult products were also in short supply. These days

A display of wartime products at Farmer Parrs Museum, Fleetwood.

smoking is known to be a health hazard and has become something of a social problem but in the war years almost everybody smoked. Pubs, restaurants and especially cinemas had to be viewed through a cloud of smoke. I can still remember watching smoke billowing around the beam of light between the projection room and the screen when going to 'the pictures'.

Such was the importance of the cigarette that the government took care to ensure that tobacco imports continued. Cigarettes were not so much rationed as in short supply and even after waiting in a long queue the smoker could not usually ask for a particular brand. Once again the black market thrived and many criminals became very rich. There was even a serious attempt made to persuade women to stop smoking in order to leave the fags for the men! I wonder how the modern woman would react to this bit of chauvinistic nonsense!

Although it was impossible to regulate, even water was rationed so as to preserve supplies for the fire services in the event of bombing. Bath water was restricted to a depth of five inches, which is hardly more than a 'stand in and splash' and families were encouraged to follow one another in or share the tub. During the blitz those whose houses had been bombed were invited to share a neighbour's tin bath but the victims were asked to provide their own soap.

Both soap and washing powders were rationed in July 1942 but you had to use the same coupons. At times you had to make a choice between clean clothes or a clean body. Razor blades were just not available and many men searched in attics or boxes under the stairs to find grandpa's old cut throat razor. Others kept their old blades sharp by rubbing them against glass, with the inside necks of milk bottles being a favourite strop.

Until 1941 clothes had not been rationed but the demands for more and more military uniforms and other associated textiles meant supplies had to be limited. Around 60 coupons per year were allocated and a man's suit would use up 25 coupons, whilst if a lady wanted a dress she had to give up 9 coupons.

What became known as utility clothing was considered to be ugly but functional, and women therefore made imaginative use of what they had available. The art of darning old socks was honed to perfection and even the eye-straining work of repairing silk stockings, in the days before nylons, was a lucrative job for some ladies.

Minnie Jaques said: 'I had lots of customers wanting their silk stockings repaired. It was possible but not easy and especially in winter ladies preferred to wear warm stockings to go dancing in rather then staining their legs brown with cold tea and drawing seams with eyebrow pencil to look posh.'

Bed linen was another luxury which required coupons and these items really were made to last. Whilst unpacking some drawers used by my late mother-in-law I found a utility blanket, which for the last two years has been part of the bed linen of my black Labrador. Despite frequent washing the blanket shows no signs of wearing out!

At the outbreak of war household goods were easily available. New cars were still available at a price, whilst cheaper items such as tin-openers, kettles, pans and even paper clips were in stock. In 1940 a Limitation of Supplies Order cut down production of all the items listed above and also included needles, garden tools, prams, furniture, toys, jewellery, clocks, buckets, scissors and even ballcocks for toilets. Cups were even produced without handles!

Those once employed in producing these items and the buildings in which they worked were diverted to make essential items such as aeroplanes, tanks, lorries and other military hardwear. In 1941 the utility scheme briefly mentioned above was developed, and extended in 1942. Utility carpets, paint, clothes, bedding, torches, lamps and even alarm clocks all had to be purely functional.

*A typical 'spiv' of the 1940s, appearing on one of Embsay Steam Railway's
Second World War Days.*

Some items such as billiard tables were not available except to the armed services and toys could not be made at all. Paper supplies were limited and the quality reduced. Clothes coupons were decreased from 60 to only 48 per year. Women's clothes had to have fewer pleats and embroidery and sequins were banned. Men's trousers were made without turn-ups and all suits had to be single breasted. A careful man who looked after his coupons could buy one pair of trousers and a vest every two years and a pair of shoes every eight months. Many a good cobbler did a roaring trade at this time! The Women's Voluntary Service and several Christian organisations set up toy recycling units to ensure that children had presents for birthdays and Christmas.

Socks could not be more than 9½ inches long. It would take seven years to save up enough coupons to buy a quality overcoat. No wonder the black market 'spivs' became rich. The fashionable 'uniform' of the wartime spiv was an advertising gimmick to prove that anyone who could dress in this way had access to good clothes and could therefore be guaranteed to deliver the goods if the price was right. The best place to see a spiv in uniform today is to visit one of the Second World War days which take place at steam railway sites. I never miss regular trips to Embsay Steam Railway, just over the border at Skipton in Yorkshire. On special days there are spivs in uniform and other people wearing 'utility' clothing. These days I arrive by car without worrying about fuel.

Nowhere was rationing more obviously felt than with petrol, the supplies of which were vital for the war to be continued at all. Rationing of petrol began on 16th September 1939, when branded petrol was replaced by what was known as 'Pool'. This was a medium octane blend. Fuel for commercial vehicles was stained red to prevent illegal use by civilians. Every motorist was entitled to a monthly ration, which varied according to the horsepower of the car. Four gallons per month was the limit for a 20-hp car, with less for the smaller vehicle. A good deal of illegal fiddling went on, with some thieves straining the red petrol through gas mask filters to remove the colour.

For those engaged in essential business, petrol coupons were issued. This applied to many drivers in the Women's Voluntary Service who were working with refugees and evacuees. Mrs Rose Davies of Oswaldtwistle near Accrington, who is still working part time at the age of 92, told me: 'I was lucky enough to have my own car in 1939 and I still have a car today. I was helping to accommodate evacuees and was given a petrol allowance to do this. The mileage was checked very carefully. I used my car when on official business but I had to go to work on the bus.' Mrs Davies had to keep her car diary very carefully and she was trained in first aid and had to attend 'invasion meetings', for which she could use her car.

Many car owners had to lay up their vehicles during the war, to prevent them being used in case of an invasion, and manufacturers such as Austin produced details of how this should be done. Some used more unusual ways of immobilising their car. I once spoke to Fred Machon, who was in the Channel Islands during the war but whose family were evacuated to Burnley: 'When I knew the Germans were coming I wrapped my car up in sacks and buried it deep in my garden. I grew vegetables on top of my car. The Germans pinched the veg but missed the car! After the liberation I dug up the car, changed the oil and the battery and it started at the first turn of the starting handle.'

But while clothing and petrol shortages were a problem, the most important concern for most people related to food. Not all items were rationed and this applied to offal, which could be used to supplement the strictly controlled meat ration. Marlene Jaques of Burnley said: 'Tuesday was half-day closing and I remember running home excited when my mother finished work early and there was sheep's head for tea. Mashed brain, sliced tongue and cheek mopped up with bread and perhaps a scraping of butter! The rest of the head made the stock base for a broth and dumpling.'

Many town councils published books of wartime recipes and I obtained a copy of the Burnley publication, dated May 1941 and costing one shilling. Proceeds were to go to the War Emergency Fund. This makes fascinating reading with the Lady Mayoress, Agnes Clegg, waxing lyrical about the wonderful taste of 'Nettles with Eggs', with dried egg used as a substitute for fresh eggs. 'Pick nettles with gloved hand. Wash them well and put them wet but with no added water into a saucepan to cook keeping the lid on. Season and serve with egg or powdered egg and just a little butter.' This dainty dish was contributed by Mrs F. Procter, the Housing Supervisor.

There were other places where good food could be obtained, as potatoes were not rationed and neither was fish or peas. When fish was available most people visited the 'chippie' as often as they could afford it. These were obviously traditional, but the British Restaurants were new. These cheap and cheerful places were set up by the government to make sure the workers were properly fed, and were run by local councils.

Gerald Rawstron of Great Harwood remembers a British Restaurant set up in 1941: 'The one in Accrington later became the Ritz Dance Hall and then the new ERA club. The meals were cheap but not very good. It was sometime later that I discovered that the custard was bright yellow and had a metallic taste because it had to be made with water and never with milk. The peas were hard and the potatoes were soggy. The meat was mainly fat and gristle. We did not go there very often.'

There is no doubt, however, that the British Restaurant, which was a feature of many places, did fill a niche. It enabled people to have a meal without having to use precious rations and it was also a place to meet up with friends. I remember in May 1941 when Barrow's first Civic Restaurant (later called the British Restaurant) opened in the Public Hall near the market. This was able to serve some 400 meals a day and operated on a cafeteria system. You had to purchase tickets before going in and you were given plastic tokens in exchange for cash. Three courses – soup, main course and pudding – were on offer but each customer could have only two. The maximum cost was 10d, which in today's terms is less than 5p. There was no choice of soup and the main course included some meat and lots of vegetables. Ginger pudding and semolina were on offer and there was tea or coffee. I remember once having black bananas floating in the bright yellow, milkless custard. Breakfasts were also available and included porridge, bread, liver, sausage and occasionally bacon. Tea, usually without sugar, was also served.

In the war years many items were used until they fell apart and even then they had to be repaired. In the cotton mills there were skilled tacklers who could keep looms working long after their sell-by date. 'A good tackler could fettle owt,' Brian Harvey of Rishton told me, 'and in the war we had to mek do and mend.'

This phrase – 'make do and mend' – was used by the government as a very effective incentive and public relations exercise. Impressive and colourful posters were produced and the concept of recycling was even more high profile than is the case today.

'Mrs Sew and Sew', a cartoon character, was depicted patching up fabrics and many an old woollen jumper was carefully unravelled. Some wool was re-knitted and sent to prisoners of war via the Red Cross whilst some squares of material were stitched together to make warm blankets. In the 1940s and even up to the 1950s many women became skilled in the production of rug mats. This required strong fingers and wrists as material was pushed through sacking using hooks. Some of the patterns produced really did brighten up the fireplaces.

Things really did need brightening up as the bombs began to fall, and a visit to the cinema or theatre, or listening to music or the radio, was an important way to forget our problems for a while and relax.

Mrs Sew-and-Sew encouraged us to make the most of what we had.

Chapter 7

Keeping our spirits up

The war years brought great changes to the whole of the North-West but to Blackpool in particular, with the requisitioning of hotels, the influx of evacuees, soldiers and airmen taking the place of holidaymakers and the departure on active service of many young people.

There was a heavy anti-aircraft battery stationed on the promenade in an area called, appropriately, The Castle. The battery took over the church hall of the parish of St Stephen on the Cliffs but the vicar managed to maintain the use of his building on Sundays. The windows of this church were huge and because these could not be blacked out early communions were conducted using just two 'sheltered' candles and in winter Evensong was scheduled at 3 o'clock before it got dark. St Stephen's on the Cliff was consecrated in 1927 and became famous as the church used by theatre people. Stars and others gave, and still give, generously to the church. As many London theatres were not functioning normally, Blackpool became a mecca for entertainment stars and most used St Stephen's as their place of worship.

Blackpool in the 1940s was a famous place in the annals of the theatre and full houses were guaranteed by the presence of troops, both British and, eventually, American.

No account of entertainment in Blackpool during the war would be complete without telling the story of Reg Dixon. Reg was a frequent visitor to St Stephen's. He was born on 16th October 1904, the son of a Sheffield steel worker, and as a lad was soon recognised as a talented musician. He had an ambition to be a concert pianist. Instead, he achieved fame and fortune on this side of the Pennines and should be listed as an honorary Lancastrian.

His early professional engagements included playing the piano for silent movies, first in his native Sheffield and then in Birmingham. Then began the Lancashire connection. He was appointed as accompanying pianist to the New Victoria Cinema in Preston. It is interesting to note that Violet Carson, who also lived in Blackpool, began her working life accompanying the silent movies on the piano. She never lost her ability, even after achieving fame as Ena Sharples in the early years of *Coronation Street*. She was a popular entertainer in Lancashire during the war.

To return to the life of Reginald Dixon. He often came to Blackpool whilst working in Preston and actually proposed to his wife whilst visiting the resort. At that time, Max Bruce was playing at the Tower Ballroom on a 2 manual 10 rank Wurlitzer organ. By 1930 the organ was not performing at all well and it was decided that changes must be made. A new organist had to be appointed and the instrument itself given one last chance.

The man appointed to this demanding post, for almost 40 years, strode the ballroom like a Colossus. His playing allowed dancers and listeners alike to forget the threats and perils of war, if only for a short time. His music reverberated in the Tower even when the top storey was being used to carry out experiments on radar. 'Mr Blackpool', alias Reg Dixon, not only played solo but he was accompanied by famous orchestras, including the Manchester based Hallé, and also singers such as Kathleen Ferrier. When the Free Trade Hall was almost destroyed by the Blitz of 1940 the Hallé went on permanent tour, with Blackpool featuring regularly on the itinerary. Before Reg Dixon died, on 9th May 1985, he recorded his contribution to *Desert Island Discs*. Among his requests, he asked to hear a recording of Kathleen Ferrier with himself accompanying during a wartime concert.

Reginald Dixon was an institution at the Tower before, but especially during, the war, but hostilities changed the focus of the Blackpool theatre. Many of London's theatres fell on hard times during the early years of the war and the losses of the Metropolis were Blackpool's gains. This especially applied to the Grand Theatre, which attracted most of the stars of the period.

When war was declared on Sunday, 3rd September 1939 the government made a decision that in retrospect seems to have been a knee-jerk reaction and which proved to be a mistake and a real threat to morale. They ordered that all theatres should be closed. This obviously caused confusion throughout the country. London actors had a problem, but those whose bookings were in the provinces had what can best be described as an additional logistical difficulty. As there were no performances on Sundays all thespians used the Sabbath as a day of travel and they arrived at provincial theatres on that day only to be told that they had no work.

At the Grand Theatre in Blackpool the cast of the murder mystery *Saloon Bar,* starring Mervyn Johns, were told that the play was cancelled. This situation was repeated all over the country, but no sooner had this silly order been given than the government began to have second thoughts. However, although provincial theatres only remained closed for a week, London's famous playhouses stayed shut for a much longer period. As the bombing of the capital increased in intensity the 'money men' became worried and most agents and producers re-located their offices, many of them choosing Blackpool. They knew that not only would bombing be less of a problem in the North-West, but there would be no shortage of potential audiences, as Blackpool was filling up with troops and also with evacuated civil servants. It was not just children who were evacuated – the Civil Service did not want to put all its eggs (ie. workers) in one basket.

Not all former actors or music hall acts could be sure of reliable employment if they lost their livelihood. Gilbert Bradshaw told me that, for some actors above a certain age, the war presented real problems. 'During the war my father, who was self-employed as an entertainer, had to give up his business, since it was geared to the holiday trade, which obviously ceased for the duration. Being too old for military service he was forced to look for a job and, having no skills of the sort required in wartime, found it difficult to find one.

Gilbert Bradshaw's father and mother in Morecambe in 1940; Mr Bradshaw had been a music hall comic all his life.

'Of course, he signed on at the local Labour Exchange. But since he had been "in business on his own account" he was not eligible to receive unemployment benefit. Hence there was no incentive on the part of the

Ministry of Labour to find him a job. There were plenty of jobs available; he told us that and events were to prove him right. But these were "under the counter" and offered only to those with proper influence (even in those days Morecambe had a flourishing mafia). The only jobs he was offered were those beyond his physical capacity, such as labouring for steel-erectors.

'Normal recourse would have been to his MP. But this was wartime and Brigadier Fitzroy Maclean, the Member for Lancaster and Morecambe, as the constituency then was, could not be contacted because he was "on active service" (he was actually doing heroic things like being parachuted behind enemy lines in Yugoslavia as Winston Churchill's special envoy, to make contact with Tito and his Chetniks; but of course we didn't know that, nor do I think it would have significantly helped my father if we had).

However, my father, who had been by profession a music-hall comic for some 20-odd years before settling in Morecambe, had knocked about a bit and was not without initiative. He took a temporary job on a rifle-range stall situated on the Central Pier at the very time that the old Independent Labour Party was holding its annual conference in the concert hall on the pier. That meant that delegates had to walk past him on their way to the conference venue. He was thus able to watch them and to seize his opportunity.

'He was looking out for a particular delegate – Jimmy Maxton, one of the Glasgow MPs, of very left-wing opinions and feared in the House of Commons because of his oratory (he had been President of the Oxford Union in his student days). Catching Maxton's eye, my father asked him if he had a minute to spare. To his credit, Maxton came over and asked what he wanted. My father briefly told him of his situation and Maxton listened; then went off to the conference session after telling my father he would see what he could do and arranging to meet him in the pier bar after the session was over.

'There, over a pint, he outlined to my father what he proposed to do. Since my father was not one of his constituents, he could not make representations directly on his behalf; however, he would have words with certain people and if, at the end of a fortnight, my father had not received satisfaction at the Labour Exchange he was to contact Maxton again by letter and Maxton would then table a question from the floor of the Commons, asking the Minister of Labour why an able-bodied man of working age was unable to find employment during a time of national emergency.

'My father did not have to wait a fortnight. The next week, when he signed on, he was received with an obsequious offer of a plethora of much more suitable jobs, from which he was able to take his pick.

'The first job my father was offered was in government service. He was interviewed, and the nature of the job was explained to him.

'At that time there was a pittance awarded by the government to widows called, I believe, appropriately enough, "Widow's Allowance". It was means-tested, and was hardly a magnificent sum. Many widows (and that included war-widows) had sons on active service, who were known to send some of their army pay back to their mothers in order to help support them, which they enjoined their mothers not to declare to the authorities. The government knew that the practice went on but would not raise the benefit. Instead they had decided to uncover these "illegal" financial supplements from widows' relatives.

'My father's job, he was told, was to ride a bicycle through the streets of Morecambe, stopping to talk to people and engaging them generally in personal chit-chat. As my father was widely known in the town that would not have been difficult. He was, however, to make a particular effort in the case of women known to be widows in somewhat reduced circumstances, when the conversation was to go something like this:

KEEPING OUR SPIRITS UP

"'Ello, Mrs Ardwick. All right, luv? Not easy now it's wartime is't?"

"No, it's 'ard times. Only get me widow's allowance to live on – and not much in t'shops neither."

"Aye, and your Charlie's away at t'war. Still, I s'pect 'e manages to send thee a bit now an' then doesn't 'e?"

"Oh, aye. Our Charlie's a good lad. Good to 'is Mum, just like 'is Dad was. 'E won't let me starve."

'At this point my father was to terminate the interview, having got what he wanted, which was an admission that the widow was, in fact, receiving an undeclared supplement to her benefit. This he would report, and an investigation and conviction would inevitably follow.

'But my father, now feeling a good deal more secure in the knowledge that Jimmy Maxton was interested in his case, thought that this was a despicable job, and told his prospective employers so in no uncertain terms. The second job he was offered was the relatively innocuous one of postman, which he took without hesitation, and he remained a postman for the rest of the war, before resuming his business when the holiday-trade started up again.'

To return to the stage, the Grand Theatre did good business at this time and all of the stars of the period stood in front of its footlights. In 1940 Robert Donat appeared there in *Goodbye Mr Chips,* and in December the Sadlers Wells Ballet with all its stars, including Frederick Ashton, Robert Helpman, Michael Somes, Pamela May and, of course, Margot Fonteyn, trod the boards of the Grand. They were under the watchful eye of the company founder, Ninette de Valois. They did not have to travel very far, as Sadlers Wells Ballet and Opera were relocated during the war to the Victoria Theatre in Burnley. Affectionately known as the 'Vic', the theatre was sadly demolished in 1955.

Bernard Shaw's *Geneva,* which poked fun at Fascist dictators, was staged at the Grand and a young man in the cast eventually became famous. Arnold Ridley had a minor

When Burnley's 'Vic' closed in 1955 it marked the end of an age of entertainment which saw Charlie Chaplin tread the boards. The Sadlers Wells Opera and Ballet were based here during the war.

role in *Geneva* but went on to have a long career in the theatre and later played Godfrey in the hit TV series *Dad's Army*. In 1944 the Grand staged *They Also Serve*, which was a comedy written by Bernard Miles who also starred in the show. It concerned the Local Defence Volunteers, by that time renamed the Home Guard, and John Hancock, born in Oldham, who saw the play as a 15-year-old said: 'If I didn't know different I would swear it was a pilot programme for *Dad's Army*. In the context of the war it was a real good laugh.'

The works of Ivor Novello and, especially, Noel Coward could always be sure of attracting large audiences at the Grand or anywhere else for that matter. Coward achieved cinematic fame in 1942 for his Oscar-winning performance in the patriotic film *In Which We Serve*. He not only directed the film but also played the part of a naval commander.

Cinemas were nearly always full and people queued around the block to enjoy a taste of what is best described as escapism. Blackpool had up to 10,000 Americans based at Warton and local folk soon stopped using the word 'pictures' and went to the movies instead.

Alan Sankey, who was born in Blackpool, became a film buff at this time and on his eleventh birthday he saw two movies which he remembers: 'I went with my mum to see *In Which We Serve* in the afternoon and as my sister was going out with a Yank I then went to their cinema at Warton to see *Gone With The Wind*, which was still sweeping the country at that time. Maybe the film was a bit long and advanced for me at the time but the huge slice of chocolate cake I was given after the show was very much to my taste.'

Clark Gable, star of *Gone With The Wind*, and other celebrities such as Bob Hope and Big Crosby were regarded as icons, casting a happy light in an otherwise dark atmosphere. Blackpool was lucky as many stars flew over the Atlantic to entertain the troops at Warton. All were popular visitors except poor old Clark Gable. Frank Thomas, the civilian designer of Warton, remembers Gable coming over and told me: 'Maybe he was off colour that day and maybe he had toothache but he cut us all short. He behaved in a way that only his parents would have loved, but then I doubt if he had any parents.' Sergeant Grant Westerman also remembers the stars who came to Warton: 'I had my photographs of Bing Crosby and Bob Hope signed but Clark Gable told me to go away, although his language was much ruder than this. He would not talk to any of us, including the officers.'

During the war, cinema audiences reached record levels and films were a great morale booster. Many leading actors learned their craft at this time, including Jack Hawkins, Richard Attenborough and the India-born Margaret Lockwood. These stars and Stewart Granger appeared in so-called 'serious' films whilst Lancashire stars such as Gracie

Tommy Handley (1892-1949). It was his being so cheerful that kept folk going during the war.

Fields, George Formby and Frank Randle kept the chuckle muscles working. Eventually it was agreed to allow cinemas to open on Sundays and an Odeon, Roxy, Ritz, Palladium, Empire or Hippodrome appeared or was reopened on almost every street in the towns and cities. In 1940 the most popular films were *Gone With The Wind*, *The Wizard of Oz* starring Judy Garland, and Charlie Chaplin's *Great Dictator*, which brought applause every time the impersonation of a ridiculous Hitler flickered on the screen. Disney's *Fantasia* also attracted large audiences and many fans would watch the first house and then join the queue for the second house and see the whole show again.

Gracie Fields entertaining fellow Lancashire lasses.

In 1941 the most relevant film was perhaps *49th Parallel*, a propaganda film about a Nazi U-boat crew on the run in Canada, staring Leslie Howard; whilst 1942 brought *Casablanca* with Humphrey Bogart and Ingrid Bergman, Noel Coward's *In Which We Serve* and *Mrs Miniver* starring Greer Garson, which was a Hollywood production of what life was like during the Blitz. I can remember my mother crying as we came out

161

of our cinema after seeing *Mrs Miniver*. We later tucked into fish and chips and had a laugh at what we had seen on the Pathe News, which told us that Germany had just had to ration potatoes. The next week we again cried at the cinema whilst watching *Bambi*, which is still a tearjerker. In 1944 Laurence Olivier's *Henry V* was a big patriotic success. The music was composed by William Walton, and Lancastrians were proud that he was born and brought up in Oldham. By 1945 there was celebration in the air and Robert Mitchum's *The Story of GI Joe* was a timely acknowledgement of the role played in the war by the 'ordinary' man. There were queues around the block to celebrate heroes such as this.

Whilst the cinema was the wartime equivalent of television, it could not go into each and every home. This was the vital role of radio, which was a lifeline for most people. Lancashire folk played a leading part in entertaining the workers during this time. A major star from 1940 to his untimely death in 1949 was Tommy Handley, who was born in Liverpool in 1892. His scouse humour appealed to all but he was also a master in the art of addressing a microphone. His voice was powerful, his diction clear and had he not been a comedian he could have earned a good living as a baritone singer. His radio show *ITMA (It's That Man Again)* poked fun at spies (Fumf), pompous army officers (Colonel Chinstrap) and civil servants who worked in the Ministry of Twerps. Perhaps the most famous of all ITMA characters was Mona Lott, whose catchphrase – 'It's being so cheerful that keeps me going' – was a battle cry for many people during the war.

John Davies, who worked in a radio repair shop in Preston, remembers how important these often battery-powered sets were in the home. John told me: 'Cups of tea were often on offer when I went out on repair jobs, and from time to time a slice of home-made cake – not many people bought cake then even if it was available. I remember during the war going to a house on London Road to repair a big Marconi radiogram, the sort where I had to remove the heavy chassis, loudspeaker and turntable even to get it in a taxi. Whilst I was struggling I heard cups rattling in the kitchen and expected the lady of the house returning with tea. She did return with a cup but said, "I've browt thee a cup o' composition, it saves t' tay." Horrible orange-coloured stuff that was foul and what I didn't realise was that it is a laxative. I spent most of the afternoon sitting on the toilet.

'Another regular customer lived in a very large house close to Avenham Park and every time I went I deliberately knocked at the front door to be told, "The tradesman's entrance is round the back." Needless to say, there was no tea and cake there. At the other extreme I used to repair several sets at Kirkland Hall, which at that time was owned by the Misses Baron. Again I knocked at the thick oak-studded door, to be welcomed by a maid who led me via a thickly-carpeted passage to a lounge. "Now sit there and Miss Baron will be with you shortly." Within a few minutes one of the Misses Baron would appear with a silver tray bearing tea, scones and home-made jam in a jar standing in a silver holder. "Now you must eat all that up and then look at the set in the dining room. When you have finished go round to the gardener and tell him I've sent you." When I saw the gardener there was always a carrier bag of whatever fruit or produce was in season.

'Tips were not uncommon, often from people who today I would think couldn't afford it. Anything from tuppence to sixpence. The Belgians, of whom there many refugees in Preston, were the best tippers. I once received two shillings from a house in Faringdon Park. Many of them were fishermen and worked out of Fleetwood; all had a picture of King Leopold over the mantelpiece. A special horsemeat shop opened in Church Street for them. While repairing a radiogram at a house in Deepdale Road I removed the back to find the cabinet stuffed with 2 lb bags of sugar. Oh, the look on the woman's face when she realised what I had found. "Er, w-would you like a bag?" Naturally during a time of rationing I didn't refuse but when I removed the sugar the fault in the set was apparent, a mouse had chewed through the mains supply cable and was suspended, shrivelled up, between the cable and the chassis.'

For many people, some huddled in shelters or delayed during a journey, reading was a wonderful distraction. With paper shortages, secondhand book shops and libraries were doing a roaring trade, but new books were eagerly awaited. As I researched this present volume I enjoyed looking for the most popular books of the period and reading them, some for the first time.

The 1940 list included two books published in 1939: John Steinbeck's *The Grapes of Wrath* (which was filmed that year, starring Henry Fonda) and *Finnegan's Wake* by James Joyce. The leader by far in 1941 was F. Scott Fitzgerald's *The Last Tycoon.* Steinbeck was also in favour in 1942 with *The Moon is Down*, but I was more motivated by the equally popular *Put Out More Flags* by Evelyn Waugh. 1943 brought Graham Greene's *The Ministry of Fear* to the forefront and the 1944 'hit' list included T.S.Eliot's *Four Quartets,* and *Fair Stood the Wind for France* by H.E. Bates. Surely no title was ever so prophetic during this invasion period! In 1945 George Orwell's *Animal Farm, The Age of Reason* by Jean-Paul Sartre and *Brideshead Revisited* by Evelyn Waugh were bestsellers.

Reading is a relaxing but solitary form of enjoyment whilst in contrast singing and dancing brought people together and fostered a real community spirit. Elsie Quayle recalled, on her 92nd birthday in 1999, that as a resident of Bolton during the war she went to a local 'do' and played the piano for the workers. Then she took out a huge pile of old sheet music and began to play for me. Her eyes twinkled and the years rolled off her and after ten minutes she looked up at me and laughed, 'We fought Hitler with tunes.'

My family were also musical with the notable exception of myself. Several uncles played in the Barrow shipyard band

and family sing-songs at Christmas during the war were a delight. I had a gramophone and still have some records I was given during the war. Metal gramophone needles were in short supply and my job was to sharpen the points using precious sandpaper, which was easy compared to using a large file – very difficult because the needles were so tiny. Hearing the songs of Gracie Fields, George Formby, Al Bowlly and Kathleen Ferrier is nostalgic today, but scratchy! During the war the wind-up gramophones were very popular, especially as they could be taken into shelters, where there was

'You can't be beat when you laugh', was George Formby's motto, 'especially when you sing as you smile.'

usually no electricity. Played loudly, they could almost, but not quite, drown out the sound of the Blitz.

The government was quick to get into the act and the *Music While You Work* programme brought famous artistes into the workplace. It also produced its own records and Eric Coates, later of *Dam Busters* fame, was encouraged to write music on behalf of the National Savings Movement. *Fanfare No. 1* and *Salute the Soldier* are now collector's items, as is Winston Churchill's disc which was entitled *The Hour is Approaching*. *The Savings Song* is self-explanatory and was recorded by Peter Yorke and his orchestra.

Once again the most popular songs of each year of the war reflected the mood of the people. What were Lancashire folk singing and dancing to in the early to mid 1940s? Without doubt, voices were raised to the highest levels in 1940 to *Hang out the Washing on the Siegfried Line* and the hit of 1941 – and the war – was Vera Lynn's *The White Cliffs of Dover*. The year 1942 brought *White Christmas* and *Praise the Lord and Pass the Ammunition* to the fore, the latter being popular even with the British, especially after Pearl

Records sold in large numbers during the war and government recordings made money for the war effort.

KEEPING OUR SPIRITS UP

Harbour. Things were getting better by 1943 and *Oh What a Beautiful Morning* from *Oklahoma* caught the mood. *I Couldn't Sleep a Wink Last Night* was sung in 1944 with great gusto by people who could remember the Blitz of 1940 and 1941. Some put their own words to the song but none of these should ever be repeated in print! In 1945 one hit was *Sentimental Journey* by Doris Day, which reflected not only the mood of victory but mourned the loss of loved ones. The fact that *Keep the Home Fires Burning* and the National Anthem were sung everywhere with gusto revealed a note of optimism and hope.

Some pessimists, writing in retrospect, blame the war years for the decline in moral standards and there is no doubt that events brought the sexes together at a very stressful time. Typically, the authorities tended to keep statistics of illegitimate births, and especially the increase in the spread of venereal diseases, under wraps. For example, we now know that more people suffered from venereal diseases in 1942 than were killed during the Blitz of 1941. Also kept secret was an epidemic of what was called 'casual prostitution', which developed quickly from 1941 onwards. An event which should not be blamed is the influx of American troops because these trends were already evident before they came – in Lancaster, for example, a long way from the large industrial areas, illegitimate births rose from 5% in 1938 to 10% in 1945, whilst the national figure rose to as high as 14.9%. However, whether sex should be regarded as 'entertainment' is a debatable point!

Care should be taken not to be too pessimistic about the so-called downside of the war in civilian terms. Far better to appreciate the wonderful efforts made to entertain all those under pressure. This is the place to celebrate the work of ENSA (the Entertainment National Service Association). The letters were sometimes said to stand for 'Every Night Something Awful' but, whilst standards did vary, some really top notch performers entertained those working in the armament factories as well as keeping up the spirits of the armed services. Ron Ormerod of Nelson said to me that, 'ENSA did a lot for the working people in Lancashire at that time. We saw and heard lots of entertainers that we would not have been able to afford to enjoy. They were there in front of us – people like George Formby, Albert Modley and Kathleen Ferrier, who once worked in the Blackburn telephone exchange before her contralto voice made her famous. So far as I know only Max Miller refused to take part but as he was a Londoner we didn't much care. Frank Randle and George Formby were more to our taste! After the ENSA professionals had done their bit, local folk, many of whom were highly talented, took their place on stage. Firms like Howard and Bullough of Accrington held their own talent contests and they even rented Accrington Stanley's football ground and after the music they arranged football matches, which often attracted large crowds.' They believed, as did many other firms, that sport was vital if people were to 'exercise' both body and mind.

All sports were played with great vigour during the war but professional soccer and cricket teams soon faded into memory. Some football grounds

Kathleen Ferrier was born near Preston, at Walton-le-Dale. Her performances during the war were inspirational, and her concerts with Reginald Dixon were part of Lancashire's wartime history.

As well as the entertainment provided by the professionals, there were smaller events taking place all over the county. Church parades like this one in Burnley raised the morale of those working in factories during the war.

were to play a vital role during the war. Bolton Wanderers' old ground at Burnden Park was taken over. In the spaces between the grandstands food for the rations was stored. Preston North End's Deepdale pitch was used as a holding camp for German prisoners of war.

All through the war, folk were prepared to work hard and they also played hard whenever they got the chance! The spirit of entertainment spread all through the community; local church, school and youth groups were active all through the war. The 'resilience of youth' is an often used phrase, but this book has been celebrating the resilience of Lancashire's civilians during the war.

When everybody welcomed the peace, the euphoria was tempered by the fact that employment would be more difficult to find and in consequence pay would be reduced. There would be hard times to come – but the German threat had been removed and we could be proud of the part we had played in bringing peace to Europe and the Far East.

Appendix

Places to Visit

Farmer Parrs' Animal World
Wyrefield Farm, Rossall Lane, Fleetwood, FY7 8JP.
Telephone: 01253 874389.

Apart from the animals, there is a collection of farm machinery and examples of telephone communications, a working siren from the Second World War and vehicles of the period. There are lots of photographs on display.

Fleetwood Museum
6-7 Queens Terrace, Fleetwood, FY7 6BT.
Telephone: 01253 876621; e-mail: fleetwood.museum@
mus.lancscc.gov.uk

The museum has displays of photographs and memories of
trawlermen during the war.

The Museum of Lancashire
Stanley Street, Preston, PR1 4YP.
Telephone: 01772 264075; website: www.lancashire.gov.
uk/education/d_lif/museums

An extensive collection of artefacts relating to the Second
World War, including mock-ups of air raid shelters and
one of the early 'prefabs' built to provide housing for areas
damaged by bombing.

The Manchester Police Museum
Newton Street, Manchester, M1 1ES.
Telephone: 0161 8563287;
e-mail: police.museum@
gmp.police.uk

Open to the public every
Tuesday, this magnificent
museum has all the police
records and 'beat' notebooks
describing the Blitz in the
city. The friendly staff
welcome visitors, and those
wishing to study the archives
can visit the museum on
other days by ringing the
curator.

RAF Millom Aviation and Military Museum
21 Holborn Hill, Millom, Cumbria LA18 5BH.
Telephone: 01229 772636; website: www.rafmillom.co.uk.

A comprehensive collection of military and civilian memorabilia, based in the former officers' mess of the camp close to the coastline at Haverigg. There are engines, uniforms, details of crash sites and civilian uniforms including the Women's Land Army, the Royal Observer Corps and the ARP wardens' kit. Despite being in Cumbria many of the exhibits relate to Lancashire and are displayed in what was the former squash court of the wartime station.

The Embsay and Bolton Abbey Steam Railway
Bolton Abbey Station, Skipton, North Yorkshire BD23 6AF.
Telephone: 01756 710614;
website: www.embsayboltonabbeyrailway.org.uk.

Much of the rolling stock and many of the locomotives date to the Second World War period. Each year a spectacular 1940s weekend is held and this is the place to see what the civilians of the period were wearing. The open fires in the station complexes are a feature on all but the hottest days of the year.

Index